T0132486

The NIGHTMARE *That* CAME *With* BLESSINGS

MARGARET GATTUSO

authorHOUSE®

AuthorHouse™
1663 Liberty Drive
Bloomington, IN 47403
www.authorhouse.com
Phone: 1 (800) 839-8640

Published by AuthorHouse 07/27/2018

ISBN: 978-1-5462-5237-5 (sc)
ISBN: 978-1-5462-5236-8 (e)

Print information available on the last page.

This book is printed on acid-free paper.

Contents

Dedication and Appreciation...vii

Chapter 1 1
Chapter 2 15
Chapter 3 32
Chapter 4 48
Chapter 5 66
Chapter 6 79
Chapter 7 96
Chapter 8 106

Closing Thoughts..111

Dedication and Appreciation

I would like to dedicate this book to and appreciation of the following:

1. My beautiful wife Margie, without whom this work would not be possible. Margie has always been here for the family and me and she continues to offer support and love when I need it most.
2. My oldest son Mark, who has always been very helpful and attentive, now a young proud father.
3. Dr. Susan Hyman, MD. Who is about as good as any doctor will ever be, she is an true Angel of Mercy
4. Dr Felicia Axlerod, MD. A living encyclopedia of the very diseases Hereditary Sensory Neuropathy and Familial Dysautonomia, she continues to give the gift of hope to everyone she touches.
5. Dr Frank Brigila, MD. A fme doctor with compassion and knowledge, he helps make the medical community look good through his work and dedication to medicine.
6. A special thanks to all of the wonderful nurses who have been here to help with our sons needs, without their help caring for our son at home would have been impossible. First names listed below:

Andrea	Sherry	Sybil	Bob
Patty	Marylin	Dianne	Cathy B
Tia	Sara	Kim	Donna
KathyT	Florette	Cheryl	John

7. The rest of my extended family for their love, support and help.

Chapter 1

My name is Mark Gattuso, Sr. I live in the southern part of New Jersey, where I grew up and still live. My parents owned a rigging and construction company and my step father, being an examiner and still as gung ho as ever, was a pretty tough guy to grow up with. He meant well though, I think maybe he was only trying to prepare my older brother and me to face life in a cold and uncaring world. After high school in 1977 I went to technical school and learned to be an Operating Room Technician. After graduating with honors, I found it very difficult to find work in the field that paid enough to live on, so my brother taught me how to drive a truck and I got a job and drove a dump truck. I earned almost twice as much behind the wheel as I would working in the Operating Room. During tech school I fell in love with a great girl and I finally felt like I was on my way to success and the kind of happiness that only love can bring. Now I would like to tell you an unusual story about some very unusual things that have happened in my family within the past 17 years. I am now happily married to the same wonderful and beautiful girl that I met in 1977 while in school; her name is Margie (she hates Margaret). On August 18th, 1979 we were married and we lived a relatively normal life for the first 7 years. Please allow me to elaborate on this because I hope to both fascinate and possibly even anger you with the details. As you may remember the early 80s were a tough financial period in this country, with the ending of a very lucrative war time economy after the fall of South Vietnam. Like most young couples we had to get by with both of us working and struggling to save, but we even managed a few short getaways before the birth of our first child, Mark, Jr. on November 4th, 1982. I was the proud father of a new son who was healthy, (yes, I counted fingers and toes) and just as perfect as every other newborn. He grew fast and did very well reaching his milestones. Then in 1983 I landed a good job with good pay and benefits. Finally it was time to reach for our slice of the American dream. I had it all; a beautiful wife who was pregnant with our second child, a wonderful son and a good job. But we had what was to be only the first of several stunning tragedies that we would be confronted with: Margie had a miscarriage during her 5th month of pregnancy and we lost a little girl, who was to be named Brandy Lynn. We cried and mourned our loss, but life for us went on. I've always been amazed by the resilience of the human spirit and the ability to "adapt and overcome."

Then in early 1985 Margie got pregnant again and would carry this child to term and give birth to a beautiful baby boy on November 5th. He was named after Joseph Cerino, who was the only grandfather I ever knew. For his middle name we chose Margie's favorite grandfather Charles, and thus he was named Joseph Charles Gattuso. Again we were on top of the world, living the American dream. As time went on and Joey was 8 or 9 months old Margie and I had some concerns about his development and what seemed like some chest congestion. We discussed our concerns with his pediatrician who told us not to worry; that perhaps we are expecting too much from him due to Mark's quick progress. He said that the congestion was probably some bronchitis and wrote some prescriptions. At the time we were planning a trip to Florida and asked the doctor if it would be wise to take Joey or postpone the trip so he could recover. The doctor thought that the cleaner air and overall environment might be beneficial to Joey's health. We took a really great vacation. We flew to Orlando, Florida, rented a car and did Disney World and Sea World, then drove to the west coast and spent two nights in St. Petersburg Beach and enjoyed the Gulf of Mexico, swimming and playing on the beach, we had a great time, like I said, we were living the American dream Joey's congestion didn't clear up after 2 weeks and a call to the doctor, so we went back and the doctor said not to worry and sent us home with some different medicine. Joey still showed no sign of improvement and now he was crying a lot after feeding, so we decided to get a second opinion. We went to a pediatrician who was said to be one of the best. This doctor ran a battery of tests, chest x-ray, abdominal x-ray, blood tests, even a sweat test to check for cystic fibrosis and we thanked God they all came back normal. Again we were told it must be bronchitis and we were given more medicine and were sent on our way. My wife and I decided that the first doctor used good old fashioned horse sense and came to the same conclusion so we decided we would go back to him for any future care. But Joey still wasn't kicking this bug and the crying after he ate wasn't getting much better. He would clear up and do well with his feeding for a week or two then it would start all over again. By this time it was February 1986 and Joey was 15 months old. Our world was being turned upside down and again tragedy reared its ugly head. But this time it was different and I didn't realize it then but life as I have always known it had just come to an end. I was being forced to learn just how dirty the game of life can become, while at the same time getting an education that no school could ever provide. February 22, 1987 started like any other day, I left for work in the early afternoon to make my deliveries to 14 different stores that would last much of the night- till about 2 or 3am. Our first stop was a store in NE Philadelphia. Upon arrival the store manager came to my partner and me (this job was made up of two drivers per team because of the extended hours on the road) and said I needed to call our dispatcher, that it was urgent. I called and was told that another driver was coming to the store to replace me, that I should call a taxi to get back to the terminal and she would wait for me to cover the expense of the ride. My son had been rushed to the hospital with what seemed to be a seizure. I got back to my car and went to find my wife and Joey in the Pediatric Intensive Care Unit at West Jersey Hospital. Joey however was awake sitting up and playing in a bed under an oxygen tent and nothing seemed to be life threatening. Margie then told me what had happened at home a few hours before.

Joey's lips and fingernails started turning blue so she called the doctor who told her to bring him into his office immediately. When they arrived he was taken to a treatment room where they met the doctor. He looked Joey over and listened to his lungs and gave him a shot and told Margie that he would be back in about 10 minutes and to stay in the room. When he came back and listened to Joey's lungs again he decided to give him another injection and Joey went into full Cardiac Arrest. Margie was frantic and was taken out of the room to allow the doctor to resuscitate Joey. The doctor then instructed Margie to drive Joey to the hospital, that he would call ahead with instructions for the emergency room and information about what had taken place. As she was telling me this I was playing with Joey in his bed and he seemed to be content; his condition seemed to be stable but he did look tired and pale. Because it was early evening and Joey had not yet eaten anything since lunch time, the nurse had the kitchen send up a peanut butter and jelly sandwich, which I started to feed him, after just 2 or 3 bites Joey's eyes rolled up and he slumped over and again turned blue. I looked up at the cardiac monitor and saw just a flat straight line. While my wife was out in the hall screaming for help, I remembered my CPR training and made sure his mouth was empty. Just as we were about to start CPR a nurse ran in and grabbed Joey out of the bed and ran him into a treatment room across the hall and as they went through the door I heard him cry out so I knew he was okay at least for the moment. I realized then that the code blue call coming over the P A system was for my son and that all the doctors and nurses that came running from all directions were coming to help save Joey's life. I realized that I had just watched my boy die in what seemed like less than a second. The minute it took before I heard him cry seemed like an eternity. A life time later, probably only 10 or 15 minutes Joey was brought back to his room none the worse for wear. After a short time he fell asleep and my wife and I went home. We called my mother to watch Mark Jr for a few days until we knew what was going on, then tried to get some sleep. We knew that we would have to be able to think clearly and possibly make rushed decisions if we were going to be able to give Joey the support he would need to help him fight for his life. The next morning we got to the hospital early and asked to talk to Joey's nurse. She told us he had a quiet night and that he slept straight through with no problems, She also said that Joey's pediatrician came in late last night and spent the night at his bedside and that a specialist would be in soon to see him.

When the specialist arrived he told us he had reviewed Joey's chest x-ray and blood work and could not yet diagnose the problem Another sweat test was ordered because the doctor thought he may have cystic fibrosis. We explained that had already been ruled out but he wanted to see for himself. After the test had been repeated and the result was again negative, the new doctor still thought he had cystic fibrosis because Joey's fingers and toes were slightly clubbed. We then told him that we wanted Joey to be transferred to either Children's Hospital or St. Christopher's Hospital for Children in Philadelphia. He told us that there were no beds available because the flu and pneumonia season was especially bad this year, this went on for almost a week. Joey's mother and I were getting more worried with each passing day, Joey was not improving and in some ways getting worse. We knew we would lose him if something didn't change very soon. Everyday we asked about a transfer and everyday we were told

4

that there were no beds. I finally decided to see for myself. Armed with some pocket change, I used the pay phone in the solarium and called St. Christopher's Hospital. I learned that with a child as sick as our son they would find room for him and I got the information I would need to have him transferred that day, this was about 4 or 5pm on February 27th. I went back to the nurse's station and demanded to see the doctor and for the nurse to start the paperwork necessary to make an immediate transfer. When the doctor showed up about a half hour later I told him that we wanted Joey transferred immediately and again he lied saying no beds were available. With all the restraint I could muster (to keep my hands off his throat) I explained that I had just called the other hospital and that! was told that a child as sick as our son had never been turned away and they would make the necessary room for which to treat our boy. He wasn't happy about my going behind his back and catching him in a lie, he almost acted like I should have gotten his permission before seeking better and more advanced care for my own baby boy. Almost like I had no authority to make such a demand. By this time we had enlisted the help of Joey's godfather George, who was also a good friend since my early childhood. George did a wonderful job helping us by watching Mark and giving Margie and me the kind of support we desperately needed during this crisis. About 7 pm that day an ambulance equipped with a doctor and nurse for a safe transport showed up, while one member of the crew got the paperwork together the transport doctor and nurse got information from my wife and I and about 7:30pm we left for Philadelphia, following the ambulance that was carrying our precious cargo, Joey. Just after 8pm we all arrived at St. Christopher's Hospital for Children, where we were met by a Pulmonologist (lung specialist) named Dr. Allen. It was a tight fit in Joey's tiny room with the doctor, nurse, Margie and me, so we gave him all the information we could and asked him if Joey would survive. All he could say was that we had a very sick little boy and that they would do their best. After Dr. Allen it seemed like the entire staff came in asking questions, doctors and nurses of different specialties, by 2 am everyone that needed information had come and gone and Joey's nurse told us to go home and get some rest, that he was in good hands and she would call if something happened.

We got back to the hospital by 8am and we were told that the acute problem had been diagnosed, Joey had a very severe aspiration pneumonia, somehow when he ate- food was getting into his lungs. They called this primary aspiration, but even worse was what they called secondary aspiration, where he would literally reflux the food from his stomach into his lungs. The acid from his stomach had burned the interior of his lungs causing them to bleed. They now had a tube through his nose into his stomach attached to suction to help safeguard his lungs and multiple IV's running along with heart and lung monitor wires attached to his little body. It was all very frightening. After Dr. Allen had explained all this, we again asked if he would survive. This time armed with all this new information he said he has less than a 50-50 chance, but he has seen worse and his chance of survival was still intact.

Because of his serious condition we asked George to bring Mark to the hospital to visit his little brother. We did our best to prepare him for what he was about to see. If the tubes and wires scared us, we figured it would terrify a four year old boy. We tried to explain to him as best as we could what to expect, but there was no real way to prepare a boy so young for the harsh reality he was about to see. All Mark knew was that he wanted to see his little brother. When he entered the room and got a look at Joey he ran to hide behind the door crying. After some coaxing he calmed down and actually began to accept what he saw. He also realized that his brother didn't seem to be in any pain, he wanted to get in the bed with him and play which he did, being careful not to disturb all the tubes and wires.

Joey had lost so much blood he needed a transfusion, so I donated a pint (they wouldn't allow me to donate more), Margie couldn't donate and our family members were asked to help by donating blood and most were ready to help. Unfortunately nobody could donate quickly enough so Joey got one pint (of S. Jersey's finest Dago Red) from me and one more pint of donor anonymous blood. After a very long 2 weeks Joey finally started to improve. But we knew it was still going to be a long battle. We never realized how hard the fight would be and how long it would have last. After what seemed like an entire lifetime- about 3 months later, Joey was finally getting stronger, his color had improved. He was fighting with all the doctors, nurses and therapists that needed to work with him. To his mother and me the fighting, kicking and crying were all welcome indications that he was getting stronger, that he was almost out of the woods. Even though he hasn't eaten in all this time he even gained some weight due to the intravenous feeding solutions (TPN and Lipids) that the nurses called the hundred dollar milkshakes.

Dr. Allen told us that Joey would need to undergo a surgery called a

Nissen Fundo Plication to stop the reflux and protect his already fragile lungs from repeated aspirations. He thought Joey was now strong enough to handle the operation and should do fine. However he also told us Joey may never eat by mouth again, that something called a Gastrostomy Tube would need to be placed during the surgery. This would allow him to get fed a liquid formula directly into his stomach, so it could not get into his lungs. We were told that the surgery would take place in about a week and that they would like some direct donor blood available for him just in case it was needed. They would like at least 2 pints but would take as much as we could supply.

Remember with little information about the AIDS problem, one thing we all knew it could be contracted through blood transfusions and nobody was sure how safe the anonymous donor blood was or how effective the new testing procedures would be to ensure the safety of this blood. Again the call for help to family members went out and we got 3 pints of directed donor blood for Joey in plenty of time for all the necessary testing to be done in time for Joey's date with the knife. The day of surgery came, they came and got Joey and after the mandatory hugs and kisses took him to the operating room. It was almost 3 hours later that the nurse came and told us his surgery was done. She said everything went well and Joey was in the recovery room The surgeon came to talk to us and said that everything went very well, that he was able to repair the defect that allowed him to reflux from his stomach and the placement of the Gastrostomy Tube had also been done and he would finally get some food into his stomach in a few days, but nothing by mouth. The day came and they tried the G-tube with a special formula and he tolerated it with no problems. Everything looked good. A few days later Joey started to run a fever and got sick, after some testing it was determined that the IV in Joey's neck had become infected, but with antibiotics and changing the IV site this cleared up quickly. We figured the worst was behind us - we were wrong.

It never dawned on us to ask what caused all of this in the first place, we were just happy he had survived this ordeal. Then we were hit with the fact that Joey still had an undiagnosed underlying disease that still needed to be figured out, that it was most likely of a genetic nature. Now almost four months later Margie and I were being taught how to feed him with the G-tube. We were also being taught what symptoms to be aware of in the future that might indicate a problem We were then forced to learn how to use an apnea monitor in preparation for Joey's homecoming. We met some new doctors that were going to be involved in trying to help each other diagnose our son. We were assured that Dr. Allen and the pulmonary team would follow Joey closely and stay involved in his care. Among the new doctors, Joey now had a Geneticist and a Neurologist to help reach a diagnosis. After four long months of uncertainty and fear, along with thousands of prayers, Joey finally came home. The first few weeks we felt like we were walking on egg shells, watching him like a hawk and hoping for the best.

Two weeks later it was time to go back to St. Christopher's for follow up care and more tests to find out what the yet unknown disease was. The neurologist, Dr. Grover, asked us to allow him to admit Joey for a two- night stay within the next few weeks in order to get a Ceryle Nerve Biopsy and do an EMG, a CAT Scan and some other neurological studies. He wasn't sure but he thought that Joey had something called Reilly Day Syndrome, which is very rare. He also gave us some information about that disease which read like a death sentence.

Plunged back into fear, Margie and I agreed we needed to know if this was the problem and what to expect. We were also told this was a genetic disease related to a European Jewish blood line. Now we thought he was wrong because neither Margie or me had any Jewish relatives, and as far as we knew, there were none in either of our family trees. We met with the Geneticist Dr. Toomey who had just transferred in from Washington, DC Children's Hospital. She told us what kind of information she would need to help Dr. Grover accurately diagnose Joey. She did agree however that this could be Reilly Day Syndrome and that it could only be ruled out by genetic family histories and the tests Dr. Grover wanted done. Dr. Toomey wanted to know about brothers, sisters, parents, grandparents, great grandparents, aunts, uncles even great aunts and uncles, anyone in either family that was blood relative. We went home and started gathering all the information we could about our families before Joey was admitted to get the other tests done, we then learned that Margie's grandmother from her father's side was of European Jewish decent. We now knew this disease that carried a death sentence was possible.

Before this admission Joey started having some very unusual behavioral problems. He started to hurt himself intentionally and began to bite his fingers to the point of drawing blood. He would bang his head violently-creating welts and bruises. Back to the hospital we went, only to learn that this is consistent with Reilly Day Syndrome. He was prescribed some medication (Haldol) that made him like a zombie with his eyes glazed and empty. Now he was always sleepy. All my wife and I knew was that we wanted answers. We weren't getting any and we also knew that any answers we did get, may not be the ones we wanted to hear.

The day came for Joey's next admission. Although we knew it was only for 2 days, we really didn't want to be there and Joey made it very clear he didn't want to be there either. We knew it was necessary if we wanted to know what going on with our son.

God only knows the kind of mixed emotions parents face when their child has an undiagnosed disease. We also knew that the tests he was about to endure may only create more questions while getting very few answers or none at all.

Day one was pretty much just getting him admitted and answering more questions for doctors, fellows and residents. While the pre-op studies were being done, we played with our boy trying to make him more comfortable and relaxed. All the while hiding from him our anxiety over the situation. The next day came and again after the hugs and kisses they took our son to the operating room to get the biopsy, which they did. Only this time it was a very minor surgery where they made a small incision only 1 1;2 or 2 inches on the side of his ankle. Through which they took a little piece of a nerve. I don't think it took a 1;2 hour before Joey was in the recovery room and again we were told everything went very well and a very suitable piece of nerve was taken. We knew that any answer from this particular test would take a little more than a week. Later in the day only 1 more test was done and the others had to be postponed due to anesthesia sickness, so back home we go waiting for the much anticipated phone call to find out what the biopsy would show.

Back at home the behavioral problems were getting worse, Joey had bitten a deep gash into his right index finger. He banged his head around hard enough that he actually knocked some his own teeth out. All the while we were calling the doctors who told us there was no magic bullet that would curb these behaviors and their best advice was to continue giving him the Haldol. The phone call for the results finally came and we were told that the piece of nerve they had taken did show some abnormalities, but it did not include or exclude Reilly Day Syndrome. What it did show was that Joey probably did not have normal pain sensation, meaning he did not feel pain like everyone else does. Now the fear of more questions was a reality. During our next follow up visit to St. Christopher's with

Dr. Toomey from genetics. She told us about a program at Johns Hopkins University Medical Center in Baltimore, Maryland that might be able to help with the behavioral problems we were experiencing. She said that she would make some calls and then let us know. She also told us that this could be a lengthy process and again there is no magic bullet, but not to give up hope.

With all of this going on the medical bills started coming in and like most I thought that our health insurance would cover all these expenses, it didn't. With my foolish male pride I thought I have a good paying job driving a truck doing three or four 12 to 16 hour nights a week earning just over $50,000.00 per year. I thought if I picked up some extra runs I could catch up, but I was not prepared for the emotional roller coaster I was about to ride. Everyday leaving for work got harder, I never knew what to expect. I would call home to check with Margie to see how things were going and was Joey okay? I remember driving two or more hours to the first stop wondering is he okay.

I knew that bad things could happen quickly, and I honestly did not know if he would be alive by the time I got home again. Remember, this was the 80's and cell phones were still a thing of the future. While I worked like an animal my wife was calling everyplace she could find to ask for assistance with these extraordinary medical bills, due for co-payments or expenses that our insurance did not cover at all. This is just the first 6 months since this disease reared its ugly head and somehow I was on the financial hook for more than $36,000.00 and bills were still growing. My wife learned from the state that I made too much money to receive any assistance (the GREAT AMERICAN catch 22). The federal government told her that there were no programs other than what the state could offer. The hospital social worker being from Pennsylvania didn't know what was available in New Jersey. I continued to work harder thinking somehow things would work out, then the collection agencies started sending letters and calling demanding money we did not have. Finally the extra hours of work and the stress of our child's disease, along with all the calls from the collectors took its toll and depression set in.

I left for work to do a trip to the Washington, DC area, it was my partner Cliff's turn to drive. As we were riding Cliff knew something was wrong, something even I could not explain. After about an hour into the trip I climbed into the bunk saying I needed a nap, but really to hide my tears. About 20 minutes before our first stop Cliff called out to let me know to "wake up". I climbed in to the passenger seat doing my best to keep my composure as I sat there silent. We did our first stop and now my partner knew all was not well with me. When we left Cliff asked if I needed to talk, he made sure I knew he wanted to help in any way he could. Finally I lost control and we talked, I cried uncontrollably because while on the road I had no way of knowing whether Joey was dead or alive, that the medical bills were out of control, that there was no way to protect our oldest son from what he was seeing and that I had no idea what to do. The one thing I did know was the harder I worked the deeper the debt got. I also knew the company for which I worked considered me a burden because they were self-insured and my son was costing them a fortune.

We got to the next stop and I managed to compose myself enough to make the delivery. When I climbed into the trailer, I realized it was loaded backwards, making the job seem impossible. When we finished I went to a pay phone and called home. When I got back to the truck I had made a decision, that this was going to be my last night there. I shared this decision with Cliff who told me that even he could tell the company didn't want me there. That maybe some revenge was in order and thought if l was going to quit anyway that maybe I should just leave from there, (Bethesda, Md.). So the company would have to find someone to finish the route that started almost 150 miles from the terminal. This would be the best place to leave from so I could catch a bus into Philadelphia and poetically screw the bosses the way they were screwing me.

We talked for a few more minutes and even though I had plenty of pocket cash to get home Cliff insisted that I allow him to give me an extra $50.00 just in case I needed it, he also gave me the name and phone number of a lawyer that might be able to provide some advice about the bills. We also agreed that he would call me the next day when he got home.

I found the bus station and bought a ticket home and while I waited for the bus I called home to tell my wife what I had just done. I asked for her to try to arrange a ride from Philly to the terminal so I could get my car, which she did. I also gave her directions to where I would get off the bus and what time I should arrive. When I got off the bus she was there with a friend, who drove us to get my car. The next day when Cliff called he explained that they could not find another driver so a manager was sent to take my place, which he thought was poetic justice considering the manager complained all night about the way the trailer was loaded.

I applied for unemployment and was denied because I quit my job, we applied for welfare, but because I quit my job, we could only get benefits for our children for the first 6 weeks. I guess I had that spanking coming to me, but the benefits we got included Medicaid for both kids. I called Cliff's lawyer friend and explained about the financial problems we had and he told me that my best option was to file bankruptcy. He referred us to a lawyer he knew that practiced that type of law. I called and it took more than a year to file because money was tight. We made small payments to the lawyer to cover the necessary fees and we had to make sure all the bills we incurred before Medicaid were in so it could all be done at once. Six short weeks later we were able to get our full benefits from welfare and I remember thinking that I should have done this sooner. Now we got our food stamp allotment increased so we could eat and money to pay the rent and household bills. Most importantly we got Medicaid to cover Joey's medical expenses. We were not living good but we were surviving. Again I remember thinking what a shame, that as long as I worked I could never afford to keep Joey alive. If i did nothing the state covered all of our expenses. To me this was wrong but I could see no alternative - that no matter how wrong it felt, we had no other choice.

Dr. Toomey called with information about the program at Johns Hopkins at what she called the Kennedy Institute. She gave us the necessary information so we could get the process started. We called and talked to their intake person who scheduled an appointment for Joey to be seen. The day of the appointment came, in October of 1987 came and we made the trip to Baltimore, MD. We arrived about a liz hour early. Once there we were impressed because rather than waiting like every other appointment we went to, they were waiting for us. In fact the man at the reception desk asked if we were the Gattuso family. We told him we were and he took us to where we needed to go. We were met by a behaviorist named Kathy and Dr. Susan Hyman. We did not yet realize that the latter would be the answer to countless prayers. After a few hours of testing, mostly psychological, developmental and behavioral and answering questions for Dr. Hyman as best as we could, we were told that they could probably help with his behavioral problems. They said that he would be put on a waiting list and told us what to expect. We learned that once admitted, we would have to be there 2 days a week, during the week, every week, for parent training until he was discharged. They explained that they had too many children waiting for a bed, rather than allow everything they did to come unraveled after he left, the parent training was just as important as the therapy Joey would get himself. They also showed us how to use magazines to create makeshift splints to use when Joey started his finger biting, so he could not get his fingers to his mouth. To us there was no question, we were willing to do whatever it took to help our son. We left for home knowing in the next 3 to 6 months we would again make the trip, only this time to leave our son over 100 miles from home, with strangers who claimed to be able to help, but they could make no guarantees beyond a promise to do their very best.

Once home we called Dr. Toomey with the information we had just gotten and started the necessary paperwork for Medicaid to cover this admission. While we waited for the letter from The Kennedy Institute with a tentative admission date, we continued with all the follow-up medical appointments at St. Christopher's. Dealing with Dr. Grover the neurologist (that had no bedside manner with parents at all and he seemed to have ice water coursing through his veins, but when it came to searching for answers he was relentless). We also noticed that when he would deal with Joey directly he seemed very gentle and caring, which was a bit of a paradox that we were forced to accept. We were told he was the best there is at any of the Philadelphia University Hospitals for children. In fact Dr. Hyman down in Baltimore knew of him. No matter my wife and I still did not like him, but we did tolerate him for Joey's sake. Dr Toomey and Dr. Allen on the other hand were honest caring doctors that left no doubt that they truly wanted to help our son. These two doctors made it a lot easier to go up there to these appointments and we even got lucky a couple of times, instead of Dr. Grover we saw Dr. Roe who was one of Grover's fellowship students. He was much nicer to deal with.

We finally got the tentative admission date. It would not be until March of the following year 1988 but with Joey ' s behavior getting worse, Dr. Toomey called Dr. Hyman with her concerns of serious injury. Dr. Hyman then managed to get the date pushed up to late January, although nothing would be quick enough, this was much better.

November came along with the birthdays for both boys, this year the celebration was very special. The boys grandparents, our friends and our family helped us throw a fun party for both boys- lots of toys, ice cream and cake, that Joey couldn't have, but he really didn't seem to mind. Maybe you don't miss something you never really had. To my wife and I this was a party that earlier in the year, we could only hope to throw, so to call it special is an understatement. Because we still had both of our children and memories we will never forget it was more than words could describe.

Margie and me now had a deep understanding of just how precious time with our children was, and even though we barely made end meet financially we managed to have a great Christmas. We couldn't give the kids many gifts, but we still had them both and we were able to share the love that only parents get with their children The gift of life, which to us at the time, was worth more than any amount of money could buy was priceless. It was then that I realized, if l had kept that good job I would have missed being with my boys and watching them grow. I also realized that if anyone in my family died, all the money in the world could not have bought back just one more minute. If l had to make a choice between wealth or family- I would choose family, that being poor wasn't as bad as living with regrets. A lack of cash was something I could change eventually, but regrets are there to stay. Like I said Christmas that year was one of the best ever because I still had my family and now we could look forward to a new year that we knew would bring with it many new challenges, most of which we could have done without.

Chapter 2

As the day to take Joey to Baltimore approached my wife and I packed for him. We carefully checked the list of things he would need and wished some miracle would take place that would just fix everything and make his stay so far from home unnecessary. Needless to say that never happened. On Jan.26, 1988 we again put our son in his car seat and securely buckled him in for the two hour ride back to Baltimore. One thing made the trip a little easier to tolerate, at least for me, he would be at one of the best medical centers in the world: Johns Hopkins, where we hoped they would get his behavior under control and possibly even diagnose his disease.

The admission process required a three day stay for Margie and me and involved more testing that included psychological developmental and physical studies. We were seeing things done in ways that we never dreamed possible; for instance they checked his hearing, which I thought would be impossible for a child that couldn't talk and had no means of communicating. They used a sound proof room with a Mickey Mouse figure hidden in a comer that lit up whenever a sound was played. They showed Joey that every time he heard a sound to look for the light. Joey caught on quickly and we found out his hearing was normal. The developmental tests were things like building blocks and nuts and bolts to see if his gross motor skills as well as fine motor skills were age appropriate, mostly they were; some of the other tests showed that he was slightly retarded.

During the three day admission process it was discovered that he was running a slight fever and if it could not be identified his stay would have been postponed. Dr. Hyman on a hunch ordered a Bone Scan because of the severity of the gash on his right index finger, and bingo there it was.

He was developing an osteomyelitis, which is an infection in the bone. Aggressive antibiotic treatment was started to eliminate this infection and because this is not contagious he was able to stay, treatment was started.

In the beginning Margie and me weren't quite sure what to think about Dr. Hyman. She was very straight forward when we talked, almost abrupt. We could tell she was very intelligent and she promised to do her best to diagnose our son. Before we would leave to go home she would get blood samples from my wife and I, for use in genetic testing, as well as personal medical histories and histories of our families. She also examined Margie and me for the basic vital signs, plus all kinds of measurements, height, weight, head size and extremities. We thought some of it was strange, but for us, it was for our little boy and we wanted to help in any way possible. She also had us sign release forms to get all of Joeys medical records and the sample of nerve that had been taken a few months prior.

I must say that the staff was something special the behaviorist, nurses and aides seemed to be as committed to the children in their charge as any parent could ever hope for. They really were professionals that took their jobs very seriously. They took extraordinary steps to get to the bottom of the behavioral problems and worked closely with the doctors to help reach a diagnosis. We were told that undiagnosed children at the Kennedy Institute was very common and part of the job was to diagnose the toughest cases. We could tell from the first day that this was a staff that worked like a team whose only goal was to win and success was the reward. They were unlike anything we had experienced thus far, most apparent of all was that they understood that communication was a very important element of their success. Up until now all the doctors and nurses at our community hospital and St. Christopher's in Philadelphia had very poor communication skills to the point that t often seemed that their right hand had no clue what was going on in their left. Margie and I were resigned to thinking this was the norm everywhere, but now we knew it wasn't. We spent time talking with the behaviorist, a very nice young lady named Kathy who tried to prepare us for what we were about to experience with Joey. We would soon learn there was no way to prepare us for what we would be forced to see and do.

Before leaving we knew that Joey would be in good caring hands, that the staff was striving to 12 reach the same goals that we were. But that didn't make leaving any easier. We had a 5 year old at home who needed his parents too. Finally late afternoon on the third day we did the hugs and kisses and while an aide kept our son occupied so we reluctantly slipped through the door into the nurses station. We stood there and watched our boy play happy and content.

The layout of this unit was very unique. The main living area was also used as a therapy and play area. There were beds that folded upward between two large stand up closets on each side, to form what looked like a complete wall. At the opposite end of the room there were two behavioral session rooms which had a one way mirror behind which the behaviorists would watch and video tape the sessions. This room was also equipped with the home style necessities like sofas and a big TV and loaded with toys of every description. The nurses station was two steps above the unit; it also had a large one way mirror so the nurses could see all the children and everything that was going on. Thus the nurses could respond quickly to any medical problem that might arise.

When we left Margie and me were silent, each trying to protect the other from our personal fears and anxieties. Which was not at all necessary because it was the same for both of us, we were equally upset over leaving Joey so far from home. When we did talk on the way home, we both cried to each other and we understood that we would need all the love and support we could share. If we were to help Mark, Joey and ourselves get through this ordeal.

When we got home my mother brought Mark home and started asking questions for which we had no good answers, but all Mark Jr wanted to know was if his brother was okay and when could we take him to see Joey. At home we tried to resume our normal routine as best as we could but with our youngest son so far from home it was almost impossible and another emotional roller coaster started. Although little Mark was dealing with the situation very well we couldn't help but worry about his emotional state too. We did our best to explain what they would be doing and he seemed happy that his brother was being helped, but he still missed him. Every day we called morning and night to check on Joey and everyone we talked to said he was just fine, adapting to his new environment very well

A week later Margie and I packed our things for our first overnight trip to take part in the parent training. We also packed for Mark, who would again stay with my mother while we were gone. It would be impossible to explain the feelings we had leaving one son to go help the other so far away, but we knew there was no other choice; we used love, instinct and commonsense to make our choices.

We dropped Mark off with his grandmother early Monday morning and headed for Baltimore. When we got there we couldn't wait to see our son, which we did, but it also meant that the work had to start as well. Before we started Kathy made sure we had a place to stay. She also told us to make sure we did something that evening for ourselves, even if it was just a walk around the Inner Harbor area of the city, to help make sure we took care of ourselves too. She made it very clear she was there to help us through his stay too.

When the work started we were to just play and interact with Joey while the session was videotaped. Then we had to place restrictions on him in an attempt to inspire the inappropriate behaviors so they could look for a cause. For his mother and I this was very hard to do, we really didn't want him to hurt himself 1f again so we each took breaks to keep things from becoming too emotional. We also saw that when the self-injury started they stopped everything to protect Joey from himself It was very painful emotionally to do some the things we had to do, but we also learned how well they could control the situation as well as the necessity of it.

About one that afternoon we were told to get some lunch and check into our room and to be back by 3 to meet with Dr. Hyman. We went into the main hospital and found the cafeteria for lunch. Then we took our car to the hotel only one block away, where we checked in, threw our bag in the room and went back to spend some time with Joey. At 3 o'clock we met with Dr. Hyman who would give us some mixed news. She gave us the good news came first, she told us that she was almost certain that Joey did not have Reilly Day Syndrome because he did not fit the genetic pattern. The bad news was that she wasn't sure what the underlying disease was yet, but we still had plenty of time.

By now Margie and me started to understand that this doctor was feeling challenged to find an answer. For her finding no answer was not an option- that in her fields of pediatrics, genetics and clinical research she would work harder than any other doctor we encountered so far to find the diagnosis. She assured us that if an answer could be found she would find it. Dr. Hyman also took the time to explain things to us and answer our questions in a way we could understand, she also gave us some advice that day that I will never forget, she said "I know Joey has problems and you know Joey has problems too, but don't ever let Joey know he has problems". Margie and I came to understand that, she was saying we should let him live and play as normally as possible. She also informed us that with our consent a dysphasia specialist (a doctor who studies swallowing and speaking problems) would be consulted to see exactly why he aspirated food when he ate and why he couldn't talk. One of her hopes was to be able to feed Joey by mouth again and possibly teach him to talk, which for us was music to our ears. We then met with Kathy who informed us that we had to give Joey some mode of communication and they would start teaching him sign language.

After a very long day we were told to get some supper and do something relaxing. Following their advice we ate and walked the inner harbor. Because the temperature was bitter cold the place was almost deserted, but it was still very enjoyable. Before going back to our room we went back to see Joey who was getting ready for bed. We spent some time with him until he fell asleep. Before Margie and I went to bed we talked and shared our feelings about what was going on We both agreed that while it would be hard emotionally and financially, it was probably the best place we found so far. We felt that here Joey's best interest came first and these people really did care.

The following morning we got breakfast early and went back to the S.I.B. Unit (Self injurious Behavior Unit) to start working with Joey. Again our job was to do things with him that would start the self injury while being video taped. later in the day we met with Dr. Hyman again who had arranged to consult with the dysphasia doctor later that week. She explained everything that would be done during this consult and had us sign the consent forms. Dr. Hyman also told us she would be contacting a doctor in New York who is an expert in children with these symptoms. This doctor was also the director of what Dr. Hyman called The National Dysautonomia Center. She would also be calling for diagnostic advice.

Dr. Hyman always made sure we understood what she was telling us, this was the only doctor we ever met that took the time she did talking and explaining so we understood what she was saying and doing. As we would soon learn she would become our greatest ally in this search to diagnose our boy. Before we left we met with Kathy who gave us a book about sign language and a short list of words and phrases they would try to teach Joey first. Most of the afternoon was spent playing with and enjoying our son. Before we left for home we asked about bringing his brother to visit and any restrictions there might be. All they said was there were no restrictions other than sickness, that if he had a cold or childhood disease it would be best to wait. Other children on the Unit may not be able to handle an infection, but if he came on the weekend we could take him and Joey out for a while and spend sometime being a family, enjoying our children together.

It was around dinner time when we left to go home and retrieve our oldest son from his grandmother, this time leaving wasn't quite as bad, but it was never easy to leave our youngest son so far away.

When we got to my mother's house to pick up Mark we were asked what was happening with Joey. We relayed all the information we had but still didn't have the answers everybody wanted. However we could say honestly that he was in the best of hands and told them everything Dr. Hyman had done and was planning to do. We also told Mark that we could take him to visit his brother over the coming weekend and he left little doubt how much he wanted to go. I also told my mother they could visit anytime they liked but if we weren't there they would be asked for identification for security purposes. We explained that we were asked for a prospective visitor list and gave the names of the people that we were allowing to visit, which was everyone we knew.

Saturday morning we left early for a day trip to Baltimore, this time with Joey's big brother who was thrilled to be going for this visit. On the way he asked if his little brother had the tubes and wires attached to him like the other hospital did and was anything they were doing going to hurt. We explained that this place was different, no tubes or wires except the g-tube that Mark had already gotten used too. We explained to him this place was more like a school then a hospital. Margie told him they helped disabled children learn to do the things that he was able to learn at home from his parents. At this place they were teaching him how to feed himself, get dressed, use a potty and simple everyday things that most kids could do without even thinking. Most of all we would learn how to keep Joey from hurting himself.

When we arrived in Baltimore we went upstairs to the unit and went right in to surprise Joey. The nurse told us if we wanted to take the kids somewhere that Joey could go out for a couple hours, provided we follow their behavior management rules, which so far were easy to follow. We took the boys for a walk down town around the Baltimore Inner Harbor. We walked around the shops and just enjoyed our family being together in the same place. We realized that Mark was learning something that we already knew, to enjoy the time you get, when ever you can, however you can because it may not last.

When we got back to the unit Dr. Hyman was there, we introduced her to Mark and she actually got on her knees so she could talk to him eye to eye. She took the time to help Mark understand what they were doing with his brother in a way that he could understand. Dr. Hyman was turning out to be someone special, she had the kind of compassion that we wished all doctors would have. Margie and I knew at that moment that we couldn't have done better any where else in the world, that our son was getting the absolute best care available.

By the time we left it was around dinner time so we took Mark to a fast food restaurant on the way back to the interstate to go home. Mark enjoyed having dinner at his favorite fast food place, you know how kids are, fast food is always better then home cooking no matter how bad it really is.

We spent Sunday doing things with Mark, trying to allow him as much time with his mother and me that we could. With Joey getting so much unavoidable attention that he was, we were trying to show Mark that he was no less important and he was loved just as much. Because he was only 5 and highly impressionable, we felt the need to do what ever it took to keep him from feeling left out. We even told him what the plans for his brother were, trying to keep him as involved as we could. After putting Mark to bed Sunday night, Margie and I once again started packing for our over night trip back in Baltimore.

Early Monday morning we dropped Mark off to stay with his grandmother while we were gone. This time it was snowing so the trip took a little longer. We were told we would be better off checking into our room upon arrival, which we did. After throwing our bag in the room we walked to the Kennedy Institute to see our son and start working.

When we got to the Unit we were told that Dr. Hyman was coming to talk with us about what she had learned. Once she arrived she was able to confirm that Joey did not have Reilly Day Syndrome and diagnosing our son would be done symptom by symptom, allowing them to rule out different diseases one symptom at a time. She explained this process would take sometime and hoped that because Joey was an inpatient they would get all the testing done and try to diagnose him before his he would be discharged.

Dr. Hyman wanted to start immediately. She told us she wanted to do a Histamine Challenge to either confirm or rule out one of the most profound symptom; Autonomic Dysfunction, that Margie and I would have to be tested as well. This was a simple test that required injecting a small amount of a common histamine just under the skin of an arm.

Because Margie has a loss of sensation on the left side of her body she would be injected on both arms, to assure the response was even due to her own deficit of sensation. They injected, Margie, Joey and me, then the doctor injected herself to be the control, this was to assure accuracy. Whatever this stuff was it made a slight burning sensation like a bee sting, but the answer was in the size of the flair, which is the redness it caused around the injection site. Both of Margie's arms as well as mine where within normal ranges but Jocy's was questionable because he only developed a small flair. They took pictures of all arms involved in the test to send to the expert in New York who now had a name, Dr. Axlerod to get her opinion. Dr. Hyman also told us that they wanted to do some other tests with Margie because of her left sided loss of sensation which also had a name, the doctor called it a Sensory Neuropathy. Dr. Hyman told us that she suspected that Joey had a universal Sensory Neuropathy, meaning he probably did not feel or respond to pain anywhere on his body. The doctor thought this would account for his ability to hurt himself so severely. Dr. Hyman also told us that a test was ordered to see if Joey could eat anything by mouth safely, that with our consent the test could be done early in the afternoon. All of this took less than an hour and it was now time to start working with Joey under the careful guidance of Kathy.

Once ready Kathy informed us that Joey was learning some basic sign language, she taught us the signs she wanted us to use while we spoke to Joey. She also explained that this time she didn't want us to place restrictions and inspire the self injurious behavior. We were told to interact and playing with him so they could see what else might cause inappropriate behavior patterns. All of this was done while Kathy watched through the one way mirror with her trusty video camera. During the time between sessions I asked why they were video taping these sessions and how the tapes were being used. Kathy explained that these tapes were reviewed by the entire team of behaviorists and child psychologists twice a week during a meeting to ensure nothing was being missed while also collaborating about the best treatment options.

The sessions were a series of short ten or fifteen minute intervals in contact with Joey. Sometimes it was with both his mother and I and other times it would be one or the other, but everything was carefully monitored and analyzed to look for behavior patterns. We were also learning how to communicate with Joey which had a very positive effect on his mother and me. Margie and I could finally start to get an idea of what he wanted and needed and for us it was the beginning of a major milestone being reached. Up until now this was a milestone we were uncertain he would ever reach.

By late morning 11:30 or so we were told to get some lunch and get right back because Dr. Hyman wanted Margie and me to see the swallowing study that was being done that afternoon. We had a quick lunch and got right back to the unit so we would not miss anything. Shortly after our return one of the unit nurses took Joey by the hand, with his mother and I in tow and walked us over into the main hospital were the test was to be done (that place is huge).

Once there we were met by Dr. Hyman and a Dysphagia Specialist, Dr. Peggy Moynihan. We had no idea what to expect with one exception, that it would not cause Joey any pain. The test was very interesting to watch, first they mixed some child friendly foods and treats with Barium and then fed it to him while watching him chew and swallow with a fluoroscope (x-ray that can record motion and movement). Margie and I watched in fascination, never imagining such a thing was possible. The results were immediate brought us great joy. We learned that Joey could eat solid food by mouth safely, but no liquids. The doctors said he would be able to drink thickened liquids and the rule of thumb would be nothing thinner then applesauce. As you can well imagine Margie and I were thrilled by this news, finally our youngest boy could eat real food again.

Back at the unit we again started working with Joey and Kathy but with the news we had just gotten left us a little distracted, but still we managed to do what was necessary. At dinner time we would get the opportunity to feed Joey real food by mouth, something we were not able to do for more then a year. Joey had some chicken, mashed potatoes and green beans. Margie and I had a dream come true, our boy was finally eating again by mouth and Joey didn't hide the fact that he too was enjoying every bite. When he had finished his supper his mother and I went to eat back at the hotel where we spent the rest of the night. For a change we were happy about the days events and what we had learned, because we finally got an answer that was good news. My wife and I somehow knew that all the answers would not always be the good news we so desperately hoped for.

The next morning back at the unit bright and early we got more good news. A special powder was being sent to thicken liquids and with a special cup Joey would be allowed to have a drink. If this was successful we would be taught how to mix liquids for Joey to drink. Dr. Hyman, Margie and I hoped this would eliminate Joey's dependance on the g-tube, making it possible to remove the tube that we never liked anyway. With all this good news so far Margie and I were beginning to wonder when the next shoe would drop, almost like it was too good to be true.

We still had a lot of work to do before he would come home again. Margie and I saw so much progress being made in such a short amount of time, it was making Joey's stay much easier for us to deal with. We also knew beyond any doubt that this stay and any hardship that came with it, would be worth the results were getting. I was also starting to realize why Johns Hopkins University Medical Center was considered to be one of the best research facilities the world had to offer. We worked with Joey under the careful supervision of Kathy and her video camera. After the first few sessions the special powder arrived and the nurse mixed up some fruit juice for Joey. She brought the special cup out to us and gave it to Joey who didn't know what to do with it. After a very short time we were able to teach him how to drink from this cup and Joey made it quite clear that he liked this a lot. After we finished our sessions working with Joey we talked with Kathy about Joey' s progress. She told us that he was progressing at a pace that they would expect from a boy with our son's limitations and she did expect that Joey would be another behavioral success story. We spent sometime playing with Joey and when his supper came Margie and I got in the car to come home.

This time when we picked Mark up we had some answers for questions we knew would be asked. We made sure Mark was listening when we told them about the test they did to see if Joey could eat and the results. We could also tell them how much Joey liked eating and drinking again. Margie and I told them about the histamine study and that the results were still pending do to Joey's limited response. Saving the best for last, we could say for sure that Joey did not have Reilly Day Syndrome, but we still did not have a diagnoses.

Through the week Dr. Hyman called to ask if Margie would consider having a Thermograph, EMG and Nerve Conduction Velocities done. The doctor told Margie how the tests were done and what to expect. My wife agreed because she would do whatever it she could to help diagnose Joey. The study was scheduled for Monday morning when we would be there for our parent training sessions.

I probably shouldn't admit this, but to keep the facts as accurate as possible I will. By this time I took a part time job under the table. I was working for my stepfather so I could earn enough money to afford all these trips to Baltimore. I worked at scrapping a large portion of a transatlantic communications cable. The work was hard and I was paid a percentage of the scrap value of the three different metals that the cable was made of, Steel, Lead and Copper. At this point every dime I could earn added up and any extra money was a blessing that helped us cover our necessary expenses.

I really didn't like doing this, it was after all a crime, but I could find no alternatives that would help us solve our financial needs. Another aspect of this job was that it fit very well with my need to be in Baltimore two days a week because I could set my own hours. I was only working three days a week and because my pay was based on my personal effort (piece work), I worked some crazy hours, ten hour days mostly. I wasn't sleeping very good because I was always worried about my family. On nights I couldn't sleep I would go back to work late at night and stay until I was too tired to continue being productive. By the end of most weeks I would earn about average $250, that was used exclusively for our stays in Baltimore, food, gas, tolls and what ever was left we used for the children.

After three weeks we had short conference with Kathy and Dr. Hyman who were working together to develop a plan of treatment. They explained some of Joey's self injurious behaviors were pretty much normal childhood tantrums that he got carried away with and the most dangerous thing he did was bitting his fingers to get attention. Dr. Hyman wanted to get Joey fitted with mouth guards that could be attached to his teeth. She wanted to have this done by a dentist who specialized in disabled children at The University of Maryland Medical Center. Once this was done the finger bitting tantrums could be ignored safely. Kathy explained that giving attention to a tantrum only reinforces the behavior there by giving a child the ability to twist a parents arm and giving in to inappropriate behavior.

Margie and I felt the mouth guards were probably a good idea and agreed provided it could be done while we were there during our weekly stays. We signed the necessary papers and the dentist came to the Kennedy Institute the next day to make impressions of his mouth and explain the procedure to us. The dentist told us that these mouth guards were very similar to the protective guards used in sports like Football with the exception that they would not come out like the guards used for sports. Joey was scheduled to have the guards put in the following Monday while we were there for our routine stay.

As planned the mouth guards were successfully fitted the following

Monday while my wife and I were there for our continued training. Margie and I were very pleased with the way the guards fit and looked.

As the weeks went by we were seeing improvements with Joey's behavior weekly. Dr. Hyman true to her word, worked diligently trying to diagnose our son. She even had world renowned doctors involved with diagnosing our son. Some of the doctors she involved had literally written the medical books about some of the symptoms and possible diseases that were being ruled out one by one.

Dr. Hyman even went as far as doing some tests that were considered to be experiential, but only if what ever they needed from Joey physically was not experimental. I remember she asked for consent to do a spinal tap to look for very specific neurotransmitters, which she would do between our weekly trips. During the following weekend we took a day trip for Mark to visit his brother and Dr. Hyman came to us to get consent for two experimental studies. These tests would be done with some leftover spinal fluid that had already been taken earlier in the week. I never knew until then that special consent was necessary to experiment with something that would otherwise be considered trash. We gave consent because we were not about to stand in the way of anything that might help shed some light on whatever this disease might be.

Dr. Hyman carefully explained what she was hoping to find, one study would look for endorphin levels in Joey's spinal fluid. She explained that endorphin was something that the human body made and that it is almost like morphine. The doctor also explained that it was a protective chemical made for things like injury, trauma and extreme stress. This chemical explains how someone can pick up something that has a child pinned and is heavier then anything that a person could lift under normal circumstances. Her hope was if he was running a high level of endorphin's in his spinal fluid that it might account for his inability to perceive pain and would have been something we could treat. The other study was to look for a metabolite of a neurotransmitter something she called Homovanillic Acid. Dr. Hyman explained how this could have a profound effect on the way Joey's brain processed information, like pain, what he saw or heard. The doctor said this would not be treated as easily, but she did believe that it could be safely treated.

We knew all along that if the disease was ever diagnosed there might not be any treatment that would offer a cure and we could still end up treating only the symptoms as they became known. We also understood that a diagnosis might only give us information about what to expect based on other cases and they progressed. At this point we weren't sure Joey would ever be diagnosed, we however were sure about how much we loved him and our unwillingness to stop trying. I also remembered as a child when my step father would tell me that when faced with a tough situation, giving up was never an option and as long as I was still breathing I still had hope. Which was basically the Marine Corps motto, adapt and overcome. Now to me I was fighting a war against an unknown enemy and there were no points for second place. The way I thought about this situation was that second place was losing our youngest son and just the thought of losing him was completely and totally unacceptable. I was determined to make sure we had no regrets, that even though life is relatively short, it is still too long to live with these kinds of regrets and there was no way we could ever just give up.

We continued going to Baltimore weekly to work with Joey under the instruction of Kathy and we were happy to see Joey using sign language to communicate. He was learning fast and we were trying to keep up. Margie did much better learning sign language than I did, she was even singing children's songs to him while using sign for the words. Margie also endured some very uncomfortable tests that were done to try to help diagnose Joey, who to her was her baby. During one of our weekly trips to work with Joey and receive parent training we got the results from the Histamine Challenge test we all took the second week of Joey's admission. Dr. Hyman told us that she spoke with Dr. Axlerod at NYU who told her that because Joey responded with a flair he should not be considered to have Familial Dysautonomia. The doctor further explained that because he had such a small flair there may be some Autonomic Dysfunction and if he did it would probably not be profound.

Dr. Hyman would call us at home once or twice a week to keep us abreast of what was being done and the results as soon as she got them. By this time she was insisting that we use her first name, Susan. In the beginning, at least for me it felt very awkward using her first name because there was no denying how hard she worked to earn the title of doctor. More than any doctor I have ever met before or since she really did deserve the title she obviously worked so hard to maintain. She truly is in every sense of the word a doctor, the kind of doctor that most med school graduates could only hope to become.

While Joey was still in Baltimore we celebrated the Easter Holiday.

Margie and I hoped this year the family would be home and together, considering all the problems that surrounded Easter last year. While the holiday could have been better and we did what we could to make it as pleasant as possible. Mark, Margie and I went down to be with Joey early Easter morning and my parents brought my grandmother down to visit and enjoy Easter Dinner at a local restaurant with us. We weren't home like we hoped we would be but we still had a very enjoyable holiday. This year was made a little better just for the fact that Joey would also be able to enjoy this meal too, that really was a nice little bonus. After dinner my parents and grandmother left for home. We took Joey back to the unit after which we headed home, knowing that we would be back in just a few short hours.

In May 1988 Joey was ready to be discharged and my wife and I were ready to have him home again and we would not miss going to Baltimore every week. Just like the admission, the discharge also required a three day stay. During this process it was more about making sure that Margie and I were ready to continue the behavior modification techniques we had been taught. I remember feeling pretty dumb for having to be taught something that I thought should have been common sense. I felt this way because with very few exceptions everything we were taught really was pretty simple stuff Kathy was able to help by telling me she spent over ten years in college to be able to teach us these simple techniques.

While everything we hoped for didn't happen the most important aspect of his stay was very successful, his behavior was under control. Kathy told us that they think the self-injurious behavior was triggered by frustration because of Joey's inability to communicate his wants and needs. They believe that Joey would hurt himself to our get attention, but even after getting our attention he still had no way to tell us what he wanted or how he felt. Margie and I always hoped to hear him say the simple words that warms a parents heart especially I love You and it may have only been sign language, but it still had the same effect and it felt just as good with silent words he was now able to use.

The experimental studies that were done with Joey's spinal fluid hinted at some clues but could not be verified. The test done to look for Endorphin's was with-in normal ranges, but the test done to look for Homovanillic Acid was very abnormal, unfortunately this was the test that was unverifiable. Susan told us that what she found was an extraordinarily high level of Homovanillic Acid in his spinal fluid. The doctor explained that this meant signals sent to his brain were probably being scattered rather than being sent to the proper centers of his brain to be deciphered appropriately. The analogy she used to help us understand was," it would be like calling our home phone and every phone in town would start ringing". Susan explained that because of the experiential nature of this particular study there was no way to know if it was a false reading and without this information we could not treat it safely.

Dr. Hyman unfortunately was unable to diagnose Joey during his stay, but I can honestly say it was not for a lack of trying. Susan worked harder than we ever thought anyone would, she made it obvious she happy about the fact that Joey was still undiagnosed. After all she worked at one of the worlds best research facilities with some of the most advanced medicine in the world available. I honestly believe it became very personal to her. We knew that becoming personally involved is something no doctor should ever do, but we also figured it is the best thing that can happen to a child like Joey. I personally will never forget her effort and dedication to our son. I also know we will never fmd the words to tell her, just how very much we appreciate everything she did for our family as a whole.

Susan also let us know she was not yet done with Joey. She did not expect us to make dozens of trips back to Johns Hopkins, but she would continue researching Joey's symptoms. Susan asked us to sign a release so the nerve sample could be sent to NYU for further review. She also asked us to consider taking a day trip to New York University Medical Center in New York City, she said that Dr. Felicia Axlerod would like to see Joey herself. Susan explained that this doctor has spent her entire career studying children with very similar symptoms and for these diseases she was the only real specialist in the country. Margie and I agreed, if for no other reason than to keep our own hope alive and continue searching for that ever elusive answer.

Susan had one more little piece of information, that was if Dr. Axlerod could not diagnose Joey the disease would probably be named after him and become The Joey Gattuso Syndrom if we agreed to this use of his name. She explained that in most cases a newly discovered disease is often named after the doctor who made the discovery. She also said the reason this might end up being named for Joey is that there were just too many doctors involved in trying to diagnose this case.

Before leaving Susan made sure we knew that she was there to help anyway she could. Dr. Hyman also told us she would like to be involved with Joey's doctors at home. She said that she would provide all the information that could possibly help these doctors to understand Joey's condition better. Susan wanted to stay involved as much almost as much as we wanted her to be involved.

Bringing Joey home was a day we thought would never come, but looking back the three months went by very quickly and was worth all the time and effort for the results our family got. Margie and I may have been happy to have Joey home again, but we also knew that there was still a lot that needed to be done if we wanted to try to fmd an answer that might not even exist. Again there was no question, we still needed to know and we felt like we owed it to little Mark, Joey and ourselves to keep trying.

After being home for a few days we called and made an appointment to visit Dr. Axlerod in New York. About three weeks later we made the trip and again we were impressed by this doctor and her staff. The waiting room had a giant bulletin board on the wall covered with pictures of the hundreds of children she has helped. She referred to these kids as her children and she told us the majority of the kids pictured had Reilly Day Syndrom. She explained that only 10 or 15 years ago most of these children would have died in their early teens and the best cases only lived until their late teens. Now with the advances made in modern medicine and a much better understanding of the disease itself, most of these children will lead full productive lives. I thought to myself so much for Dr. Grover and his outdated, obsolete information.

Margie and I quickly learned that Dr. Axlerod had many of the same qualities that made Dr. Hyman so special. She too exercised compassion and understanding along with the patients to listen to our concerns, while making sure we understood what she was telling us. While we were talking with the doctor we asked about the nerve sample sent from Baltimore and she had gotten the chance to look it over. Dr. Axlerod told us that she had never received it and that she would be looking into it's whereabouts. She did assure us that as soon as she got the specimen that she would personally review it.

Dr. Axlerod ran some strange tests in her office and got blood samples from all of us for DNA analysis and to be listed with the very new Human Genome Project at the National Institute's of Health in of all places, Bethesda, Maryland (were I quit my job almost a year before). By the time we were ready to leave, this doctor was just as perplexed as all the other doctors before her. Dr. Axlerod told us that there was no simple answer and the variety of symptoms did not fit with any disease she knew of. She also told us she would send a report to Dr. Hyman in Baltimore and any other doctors we specified. Dr. Axlerod gave us phone numbers (including

30

her home phone) by which to reach her for any reason, she also told us she would like to stay involved in Joey's care. Margie and I realized how fortunate we were to have found the caring professionals we have found to help Joey. Dr. Axlerod also became an important ally in our quest to secure a future for Joey. When we got home from New York it was too late to call Susan with the information we had gotten from Dr. Axlerod. First thing the next morning I called Dr. Hyman to share our information. I told her that Dr. Axlerod could not find any answers based on the clinical information she received from her along with the list of symptoms and tests she did while we were there. While on the phone I asked about the nerve specimen that never showed up at NYU and she said she would have the package traced and let us know what happened to it. About a week later Susan called to tell us the package had gotten lost, Dr. Hyman was very apologetic and hoped it would be found. She also said what a shame it was to lose such a beautifully preserved piece of nerve mounted in wax, ready and waiting to be studied.

I was somewhat stunned by the phone calls we were getting from Kathy and her team of Behaviorists to check on Joey and us. For the first few weeks they called twice a week and then weekly. I was really shocked to see how much caried they about the work they did. Kathy and another team member actually came to our apartment six weeks after Joey was discharged. This validated my opinion of these people, they were all professionals of the highest caliber. All this was done to make sure Joey did not relapse and that we did not need to learn more techniques to keep the self injurious behaviors under control.

Everything was going well, maybe even too good. Margie and me had no clue what was headed our way or the roll Dr. Hyman would play from over 100 miles away in the coming months. Margie and I weren't sure where to go or who to see at this point to continue our quest to find a legitimate diagnosis for Joey. We did know however, without a formal diagnosis we would never know what to expect or how this disease might progress. We weren't even sure we should continue trying to find answers for something that never even existed before Joey's birth, to us it all added up to confusion and uncertainty. On the bright side we did have more information to work with and some of the best doctors in the world to help with Joey's problems and lend guidance to my wife and I. We never knew how much more difficult the challenges would become, nor could we begin to imagine the blessings we would receive along the way.

Chapter 3

By now with Joey's stay in Baltimore well behind us, we continued our lives as normally as possible. We were thrilled with all the improvements in Joey's overall quality of life. His behavior was under control and he now had a way to communicate his needs. Best of all he was able to join us at the table for meals and eat normally. Margie and I took these things for granted with Mark, but now we had a deep appreciation for some of the smallest things in life. The changes were so profound that we felt like we had been given a very special blessing.

Summer was approaching rapidly with all the new life Mother Nature brings with it. To our family this was a very welcome season because we enjoy a verity of outdoor activities. Margie and I always liked cookouts, walking in the woods, fishing and swimming. Our favorite summertime activity was go to the Jersey shore because we loved to swim and play on the beach in Cape May. When it would get to be around dinnertime we would go to Wildwood to walk the boardwalk and take the boys to the amusement piers for the rides. Before coming home we would buy the mandatary items the Jersey shore has to offer, Saltwater Taffy and Fudge.

My wife and I believed the worst was behind us now and hoped we could look forward to some normalcy in our lives. We had no clue how wrong we were. Joey was only home about two months before tragedy would strike and threaten the life of our youngest child again.

I don't remember the exact date, but on a Saturday in mid June of 1988- Joey had an episode that scared us more then any before. I was home with Mark and I got a phone call from my wife, I knew right away that something was wrong and I could tell by her voice she was very upset almost frantic. Margie told me to call our neighbor to watch Mark and come to Kennedy Hospital right away. When I arrived she told me that Joey had stopped breathing and turned blue while she was driving home from the store that she had just left. She pulled into a gas station and asked the attendant to call an ambulance. Then she pulled her baby from his car seat, she laid him across the hood of the car to start mouth to mouth resuscitation. Fortunately the ambulance was only a few blocks away because they were returning to their station following a very recent call, so she had help in a matter of seconds. All of this had just happened and the emergency room doctors could not even begin to tell us what had happened. The doctors and nurses were still very busy treating Joey who was now breathing on his own, but still needed medical attention.

Joey had a fever of 106° which made no sense at all because he was fine, not so much as a sniffie earlier in the day. Because of the high fever he was iced down to reduce his body temperature, they started an IV and hooked him up to the heart -lung monitors. One of the doctors told us the most common cause of this sudden condition is Meningitis so Spinal Tap was done to check for this potentially fatal disease. The results of the spinal tap came back rather quickly and we thanked God they were negative, but it also meant we didn't have a clue about what caused this to happen. After he was stable we asked the doctors if he could be transferred to West Jersey Hospital because the nurses there were familiar with him. We also felt that Joey might be more comfortable where the people he encountered were somewhat familiar to him. Within the first hour Joey's body temperature had returned to normal and he was transferred as requested.

By the time he got to West Jersey Hospital he was doing very well, but his Pediatrician wanted to keep him overnight for observation. After what had just happened we felt this was probably a good plan and agreed wholeheartedly.

I called Susan Hyman back at Johns Hopkins to ask for advice, again this lady was ready to help in any way possible. I did my best to explain what had happened, after which she asked for the name of the attending physician and a phone number to contact him. Before hanging up we made arraignments to talk later that day. As soon as I finished talking to her she called and talked to his treating physician and got as many details as she could along with all the clinical data obtained from this admission so far. Joey's doctor admitted to her that he had no idea what had caused these bazaar symptoms that almost claimed the life of our youngest child. The doctor also agreed to cooperate in any way possible hoping to understand what was happening to his young patient.

Later that day as planned Susan and I spoke but she too was at a loss for an explanation. She did promise to do some research based on the symptoms to see what she could find. Susan also told me that with a disease that has never before been encountered, these things may happen and for now the best we could do -was to treat the symptoms as they became known. I wasn't really happy with the answers I got, what parent would be? I knew I could trust this doctor and if this problem could be figured out Dr. Hyman would most likely be the doctor to find the answers.

I almost felt like I was living a sick nightmare that had lasted more then a year that I could not wake up from. I remained positive that somehow everything would workout and hoped unrealistically that Joey would just out grow these problems and he would be okay. Nothing could have been further from the truth; but somehow I talked myself into believing these lies I was telling myself I also had no idea what kind of damage this false hope would cause me personally. As you will see later denial can be a very dangerous thing.

Sunday morning the doctor at West Jersey Hospital could see no reason to keep Joey any longer, so he was discharged. We were told to keep a close eye on his temperature and breathing effort. He said that ifhis temp went above 100° or if he looked like he was having trouble catching his breath to call him immediately and then take him to the emergency room. He really didn't have to tell us this because Joey would be living under a microscope with us and his every move would be watched very closely by his mom, dad and big brother.

Again we were walking on egg shells, wondering what would happen next. Margie and I also had another problem Our oldest son who is healthy in every way and we knew it wasn't fair to limit his activities because we were so worried about Joey. Acting on instinct we took turns doing things with Mark. Margie would take Mark to the pool for an hour or two then we would switch. We also called George to ask for his help, but because it was the busy season at the Scuba Diving store he managed his time was very limited.

George is an avid scuba diver and instructor, so when time permitted he would take Mark out on the dive boats he worked with. Between dives he would get in the water with Mark and teach him how to be safe in the ocean. George taught Mark the different techniques to swim and float for long periods of time in case of an emergency. He was also teaching him all the things divers must learn before being certified. He also taught him how to snorkel which Mark loved and when they were able Mark did some fishing which was also very special. Being a father I would have liked to be there with my boy, but I also knew that our situation at home with Joey was very touchy. There was no way I could have left Margie alone, knowing there would be no possible way of contacting me in case of an emergency.

Because George lived at the shore there were times when he would pick Mark up for the weekend to go to the beach and show Mark how to use a Boogie Board in the sur(Mark liked it so much George even bought him a board of his own and a wet suit. In the evenings he took Mark fishing from the jetties and surprised him by the number offish they could catch so close to the beach. Mark also found out how good fish tastes when you catch it and cook it that fresh. In a lot of ways George helped with our oldest son. He used to joke about how nice it is to rent a kid have fun with and then bring him home for the task of parenting.

On the 41h of July it was a typically hot humid summer day in New Jersey, with the temperature in the high 90s. We were hoping to have a nice cookout with some family and friends and take the boys to the fireworks that night. Then as if the nightmare wanted to cause more torment, it happened again. Mark was at a parade with some friends and their children, I was in the kitchen getting the chicken and ribs ready to marinate. Margie took Joey to her parent's house to visit her father who was slowly dying from Lung Cancer.

On her way home it happened again, this time she was stuck behind some fire trucks bringing up the rear of a small parade in the town where her parents lived. Joey slumped over blue and not breathing in his car seat. Margie got the attention of the firemen on the truck in front of her for help. They had an ambulance in their company who broke from the parade to care for Joey (blessing #3). This time it was worse because his heart stopped and he was again clinically dead for a very short time. Fortunately the EMT on the ambulance was able to resuscitate our son quickly while they rushed him to the hospital. When he arrived at the hospital he had a fever of 1 06.7°. Margie called me crying and I went right over, this time he was taken to Underwood Memorial Hospital which is only minutes from where this happened.

Joey's little body was iced down an IV was started along with all the monitors hooked up once again. This time we told the doctors that we wanted him transferred to St. Christopher's hospital in Philly as soon as he was stable enough for the trip. Margie and I were afraid we were going to lose our son to one symptom that we could not control. We also knew he needed the best medicine available in our area for him. This was a fight we were not prepared to lose. I tried to contact Susan in Baltimore but she was away for the holiday. Our son was sent to St. Christopher's within an hour or two and we hoped this time we might find out what caused this recurring problem.

By the time he arrived in Philadelphia his temperature was again normal but the doctors did another Spinal Tap anyway to check for Meningitis which was negative, which left them scratching their heads. Joey was admitted to stay the night for observation and just like the last time, he was discharged the following morning. Margie and I were beside ourselves with fear because we didn't know how to protect Joey from this invisible threat. We also wanted to protect Mark from what was happening with his little brother and being shuffled around to different baby sitters and grandparents, but we could find no other solutions.

July 61h Susan returned from her short trip and got my message. She called me early in the day and we did some brainstorming. Reaching for straws I asked if Joey might be reacting to the hot, humid summer weather. This was something we had not considered before because he didn't have this problem during the two previous summers. Dr. Hyman thought it couldn't hurt to check and explained what to do. She told us to take Joey to the pool with a thermometer so we could monitor his body temperature closely. If his temp started to rise to put him in the water to cool him down and then check again a few minutes later. She said to repeat this process several times and if it was the air temperature causing this problem we would be able to find out by following these simple steps, Susan also asked us to call her back with our findings.

Until now we had been keeping Joey indoors as much as possible for fear of something happening that we would be unable to control and not being near a phone to call911 for help. Following her advice we went took Joey's temp at home before we left. We then went to the pool with both boys and our trusty thermometer. Once there we kept a very close eye on Joey, after ten minutes we checked and sure enough his temperature started to rise. After a short soak in the pool his temp was again normal, as instructed we did this several times with the same result every time.

As requested I called Susan back and explained what we did along with our results. She told me that we may well have found the problem along with a treatment. Being cautious she also told us that every time we took Joey out in the heat to make sure we had thermometer and a cooler full of ice water. We told to keep a close eye on his temperature and if necessary to soak him with the ice water. Margie and I did as instructed and this particular problem never reappeared. Finally we were able to effectively treat a symptom that allowed Joey a more normal lifestyle. This may have only been a very small piece of a much larger puzzle but for us it was victory pure and simple. It was also a major blessing we could add to the list of problems we were able to help Joey to overcome.

Because of Joey's lungs were already fragile he always required treatment both at home and when necessary in the hospital. Margie and I were getting good at detecting symptoms before a major illness set in. Unfortunately we were also getting used to Joey's need to be admitted to the hospital for a bad cold or pneumonia. Although we could have lived without these hospitalizations, they were a necessity Joey could not live without. We looked forward to the fall when the hot weather would begin to subside. We were also looking forward to being able to leave the thermometer and ice water behind every time we went out. I really am amazing by how quickly attitudes can change. As much as we loved the warm summer weather, we now wanted the cooler days of the fall and winter.

It was during the month of July when I got a call from the New Jersey Department of Special Child Health Services. The case worker named Becky, that we never even knew existed wanted to know when I was going to return to work. I told her I was never going back to work as long as Joey required outrageously expensive medical care because I could never afford to keep him alive. Becky told me about a program in New Jersey called the Division of Developmental Disabilities (DDD) that would supply Medicaid for our son as long as his medical expenses exceeded 10% of our total net income. At the price of Joey's care this meant I could literally have a multi million dollar income and Joey would still have been eligible to receive medicaid. I asked where was this pro gram before I gave up a $50,000.00 per year job; her response was they must have forgotten to tell us about it and she was sorry.

I instantly learned another valuable lesson was learned which to me was very tough pill to swallow. I now knew beyond any doubt that I could not even trust my own home state to make programs available that might help Joey and our family. To say this information left me feeling enraged would be a gross understatement. I just could not believe the state I lived in and paid taxes too had totally betrayed us this way. Worse yet they defrauded a medically fragile child and his family out of information about programs that the federal government had already paid for. I felt like · someone owed me the money I could have earned from career that I had been forced to give up based on some state employee's total lack of interest and their personal inability to care.

I called an attorney for the first time in my life and asked about a possible lawsuit against the state of New Jersey for not disclosing information about possible entitlements as required by federal law. When I sat down and talked to this lawyer and told him about what had happened he taught me just how naive I had been. The attorney explained how when the state caught their mistake of not disclosing the information about DDD they had to wait until my statute of limitations had expired to avoid this lawsuit. He told me that had I learned about DDD sooner I would have had a very strong case. As if to add insult to injury, he told me this was not first time he has seen this state do the same thing to other families that came before. I really had a tough time believing what this attorney was telling me; it just sounded too cynical. It was all so unbelievable that I needed to get a second opm1on.

Unfortunately the second lawyer basically said the same thing, he too had seen this before. The best advice he could give was to try to make a contact inside The United States Healthcare Finance Administration (HCFA), he also explained me how I might accomplish this. To this day I cannot begin to tell you how bitter this left me toward the State of New Jersey. To commit such a crime against a child which left no recourse due to their careful legal calculations was beyond reason. I couldn't believe how easy it was to establish a contact within HCF A. I simply called and explained what our experience had been with our state to the operator at HCFA who connected me with a wonderful and helpful lady named Jane. I found that as long as I sounded like we were in need of help, she would give me all the information I needed to secure Joey's entitlements. After all this was the federal agency that gave the money to all 50 states for these programs that were created to help disabled children. Jane also told me that there were a few states that commonly did this and New Jersey was one of them. She also said that while this made her sick, HCFA had no authority to enforce the federal mandates. Jane sent me a packet of information that was about two inches thick which contained helpful information that I hadn't even thought to ask for. I was also able to add Jane to our list of allies. I got an extremely valuable education from this kind and caring lady. We talked often and I learned more with each conversation, most important was not to be afraid to ask our Congressman and Senators for help.

Because the state was giving us a hard time about the Welfare they forced us to collect because they failed to disclose the information that could have saved me from quitting my previous job. Margie got a job and learned to drive a school bus. The bus company provided all the necessary training for her to get her license to drive a bus and she would start working in September 1988 at the start of the new school year.

As November approached we planed another Birthday party for the boys and this year Joey would be able to enjoy some of his Birthday Cake that he missed the year before. We also planned a special Thanksgiving Day Celebration unlike any before. This year we had even more to be thankful for. Joey would enjoy his first Turkey dinner complete with all the trimmings and eat with the family. Margie and I were especially thankful to still have both of our children home and alive. We were able to understand better then ever before how much we had to be thankful for and how quickly it could all be lost.

By the time winter came and after some job counseling provided by New Jersey through The Department of Vocational Rehabilitation because I refused to drive a truck again. I was told that because I had an education I could fall back on, having trained to be an Operating Room Technician after high school they would only help me become ready for a job in that field. I was very happy to learn that the wages for this job had increased dramatically to more than twice what it paid when I graduated tech school back in 1978.

I got job counseling through the fall and Vocational Rehabilitation was able to make arrangements with a local community hospitals Underwood Memorial Hospital to give me a chance to update my skills. The state offered to reimburse the hospital 50% of my wages for the first six months provided they gave me full-time employment that led to a permanent position. I got the job and looked forward to entering the workforce again. I would have to wait until after the New Year to start my new job and career, but to me it was like an early Christmas present.

Margie had a job she loved and I would be starting a job very soon so as Christmas approached we were able to appreciate the season more then ever. We were still living on a very tight budget, but we still found a way to give our children a wonderful Christmas. Mark was a real trooper because at only 6 years old he was developing wisdom far beyond his years. He understood that there is more to Christmas then receiving toys and gifts, he also understood that his little brother's survival was a gift to the entire family and he knew just how valuable that gift was.

Like every year before the Christmas season brought the New Year with it. Margie and I were grateful that a year that brought so many trials was now behind us. We also knew the New Year would most likely come with more challenges, we still hoped it would be better then the year before. Margie and I were still trying to find a way to solve all of Joey's problems by researching anything we could, hoping to find some answers. We also began to realize that we didn't know what to expect with any one of us, that bad things happen for no apparent reason. We knew from past experiences that good people can die unexpectedly. It happen with my grandfather who died because of a Heart Attack at the age of 71. As I looked back through my life I remembered family friends that were killed in Vietnam. I also remembered the times in high school when I lost friends to accidents and even a few to drug overdoses. While it may not make much sense the reality is that a lack of expectations with Joey actually made things a little more normal.

We expected Mark to do good in school grow up and get married and start a family of his own. We also knew not to expect the same from Joey, we knew he was developmentally disabled and he would require more help with education and common goals. To us this is what we could expect and without knowing how Joey's disease would progress we didn't know what the future would bring. To us this actually made our lives a little more normal because we didn't know anything about anyone else's future either. Like the rest of the world our Crystal Ball was broken too, which means we would have to wait to see what the future will bring like everyone else. It never took long before future challenges were revealed, most of the time they came too quickly.

Margie's father who had been battling Lung Cancer and Congestive Heart Failure passed away on January 131

\ 1989. Two days later on January 151

\ 1989 I received a call that Margie's sister

Robin was just killed in a very bad automobile accident. I received this massage while my wife was on her way home from work. By now I thought I had already done the hardest things I would ever do because of what we had already endured with Joey. I figured I could never be faced with a tougher task, until now that is. I had to do something that I wouldn't wish on my worst enemy; I had to fmd a way to tell my wife what had happened to her sister. All I think of was that I love my wife so much how could I possibly give her information that I knew would only cause her great pain and anguish.

When she got home from I somehow found the strength to tell her about Robin's death, that I had only received the call fifteen minutes prior to her arriving home. Margie made some phone calls to fmd out where her sister had been taken. She called Kennedy Hospital and was told Robin was there, she was also told that we should go there right away. We got a sitter for both boys and went to the hospital as soon as we could. When we arrived we were taken to a room where we were asked to positively identifY her sister's body.

Robin was the only girl in a set of fraternal triplets, the other two were boys, Charlie and Bill. As it turned out Bill was one of the EMT's that responded to the accident, worse still Bill happened to be the EMT that found Robin on the scene. Bill was taken to a hospital to get help for the shock he suffered due to his grizzly discovery. Because of the circumstances of Robins triplet brother making this find and the shock it caused the hospital personnel wanted our verification in case Bill was mistaken.

Then on January 16¹ h came and Joey caught a bad cold and from past experience and the way life was playing out we knew not to wait before seeking medical attention. We knew it probably meant another hospitalization but we were not taken any chances. Joey contracted a virus referred to as RSV (Respiratory Syncytial Virus) which generally causes Bronchiolitis in people otherwise healthy. In people like Joey who already have damage in their lungs this can cause a particularly bad pneumonia, which it did to our son. Fortunately we caught the symptoms early which enabled the · doctors to successfully treat our son.

Beginning Monday the following week it was like a nightmare that would have made Stephen King proud to write about in one of his horror stories. We had four days straight of viewing's and funerals, the first two days were for Margie's father and the next two days were for her sister. To call it a week from hell would be an understatement. I only hoped my wife could forgive me for being the person to deliver such horrible news that caused her so much emotional pain. George was asked to keep Mark busy and being the faithful friend he is came and helped. To this day I can't :find the words to express our appreciation for all his help with our oldest son during these times of need.

Once again Joey was a very sick little boy with mom and dad by his side. The first few days our little boy only three years old, didn't want anything to do with anybody or anything. He slept most of the time and when he was awake, he was miserable. While Margie and I were quite worried, we took comfort in the fact he was fighting with everybody that needed to work with him. The respiratory therapist had the most trouble because Joey didn't want the treatments they needed to give him. Parents always want there children to be little angels and cooperate with things that are meant to help, but somehow his fighting seemed appropriate under the circumstances. To his mother and I he was fighting to survive which needless to say is what we needed to see.

During Joey's ten days in the hospital something unusual happened, we were contacted by one of our local TV news stations. Channel6 Action News wanted to do a story about Joey and his disease that has been named for him. We agreed and they made all the necessary arrangements with the hospital for a news crew to come out and interview Margie and I with Joey. It was kind of exciting to have gotten the attention of the news media, at the same time it was also intimidating to give up our privacy on camera.

The interview was done two days later and Joey was just starting to respond to the treatment but he was still tired and weak. During the interview he was held in his mother's loving arms and we answered all the questions in the best way we could. The news anchor was a very nice lady named Cathy who was careful not to expose the private information that concerned us. She somehow made Margie and I very comfortable with what we were doing.

Because of the extensive research done at Johns Hopkins Medical Center we were asked to allow them to interview Dr. Hyman in Baltimore pending her approval. I called Susan and asked if it would be okay to give her contact information to Cathy, she approved and was contacted that day to schedule an interview with her in Baltimore.

Before the news crew left we asked when this story would air. We were told that because this was not breaking news, it might be a few days before we would see the story on the evening news. Cathy promised to call us as soon as she knew it would be on TV. Two days later we received a call from the Cathy telling us the story would be on the 6 o'clock news that evening, she also said it might air again at 11 o'clock if it didn't get bumped by other news. Margie asked me go home for the news so I could tape it on the VCR, to which I agreed.

I got home in plenty of time to copy the story and was pleased with the way the story was done. I'll never forget the description Susan gave for Joey's overall disease, she said that" it is as rare as hens teeth", that based on the genetic pattern and the symptoms this is a disease that never existed before Joey came along. While I watched this on TV I was reminded how much of a privilege it was to have Susan for an ally to help with our son.

After ten days Joey came home and life continued in the only way we now knew. Throughout the rest of the winter our son would find himself in the hospital two more times for pneumonia or related illnesses. We were proud to see that just like his parents who would never stop fighting for their son; Joey continued to fight and beat everything life would throw at him.

It was time for me to start my new job in the Operating Rooms at Underwood Memorial Hospital, doing a job I had only experienced during the internship phase of my training. I was very excited to be gainfully employed again, but I was also somewhat nervous about my skills and the work I would be doing. I was also surprised by how quickly everything I had learned in school came back to me, almost like riding a bicycle. I got along very well with the staff who offered support for my family and everything we had been through. This hospital had six operating rooms for all surgeries and one short procedure room for minor surgery and for the most part all the rooms were constantly busy.

Spring time was coming quickly but unlike little Mark, Margie and I weren't looking forward to the hot, humid weather ahead. We had too many bad experiences with the heat last year and we were afraid of what it might do to Joey this year. We also knew that with hope comes blessings and they always seem to hide in places you would never expect to find them.

We happened to be watching a TV show about how modem technology helps people with disabilities, only this show gave us information that might help Joey handle the summer heat. It was about a boy born without sweat glands and how the company that manufactures the Space Suites for NASA, built a special vest and helmet to help keep this boy cool. The show also gave the implications of a person trying to cope with the hot sunlight and heat without the benefit of having sweat glands to help cool a person and protect their skin. I was sitting there thinking about Joey and how something like this might benefit him. I sat there trying to figure out how to get more information about this equipment. I also knew the price would almost definitely be out of reach, but I still knew if it could help Joey we would find a way.

We don't know how, but Joey's name was given to the Sunshine Foundation to receive a wish and out of the blue we were contacted. Margie and I spoke to a very kind lady who represented this foundation named Betty who asked about granting Joey a wish and what would he want. I made sure she knew that Joey's condition was never considered terminal and she told us that was not a requirement to be given a wish (I always thought it was only for children with terminal diseases). I explained about that TV show and the vest and how it was able to help another boy. We thought if they could get Joey a cooling vest like the one on the TV show, it would probably be the one thing Joey would want most. Betty took the information and told us she would see what she could find and call us back. She also gave us a phone number where we could call her in case we changed our minds or found something else.

About a month later the Betty called to tell us she had no luck finding this equipment that we had wished for Joey. I told her I would make some calls to see what I could find and call her back. The only place I could think of calling was NASA but I was told that they would not even consider talking to common working class man like me. I had nothing to lose but time and the price of the call, so I tried. I called information for the phone number to the Goddard Space Flight Center in Greenbelt Maryland (this was closest to our home). The only reason I even knew about Goddard was because I made deliveries to a store across the street from their main gate.

I called and asked to speak to someone in their Public Relations Department, which was answered by a very accommodating young man. I asked if he could tell me who the contractor was that made the Space Suites for NASA. He told me they would not have that information and told me to call NASA Headquarters and gave me a phone number. I called NASA Headquarters and was told they didn't have that information either, they told me to call Johnson Space Flight Center in Houston Texas and gave me that number. I called Johnson Space Flight Center in Houston who told me the Space Suites were manufactured by ILC Dover in Dover Delaware and gave me their phone number.

It turns out that Betty from The Sunshine Foundation spent a month calling everywhere except NASA and found nothing. I spent less then an half hour on the phone and got the information we were looking for. I also learned another valuable lesson, never to be too intimidated to make a call or ask a question because of my own ignorance of what I'm trying to do or find. I also learned that these people that work in the world of modern technology love to help, especially children. I called ILC Dover to get some information about the vest we were looking for and the operator connected me with a very helpful young lady named Rhonda. I explained what we was trying to do and she told me they had never made such a device and knew nothing about what we saw on TV. Rhonda did say however, that all they would need is very specific measurements to make something to do this job. She told me exactly how to measure Joey and asked us to get the measurements while we were on the phone. After we gave her all the information, she got our phone number and told me she would call us the next day to tell us what they could do for our son.

As promised Rhonda called and told us their company was in the process of making cold fracture splints to be used by ambulance crews around the world. She explained that they have several prototypes being tested by select Emergency Squads, that with Joey's small size she wanted to send a large adult size thigh splint for us to try with him. We accepted her offer and received the splint a week later. I called the Sunshine Foundation and explained what was going on and Betty who I had been talking to could not believe that NASA had been so helpful.

By the time I found the information it was already getting hot during the day and the arrival of the package from ILC Dover was a very welcome addition to Joey's equipment. The splint was a three piece gadget. It was the splint that we could wrap around Joey's torso that closed with Velcro, which was connected to a small oox that contained very Hi-Tech machinery. These two pieces were joined together by a group hoses in-between. The device ran on a very small battery that would run the unit for 4 or 5 hours and this thing was very light weight.

The frrst time we tried this device in a real world situation was at home playing outside our apartment. We did this in case it didn't work as well as we hoped and Joey started to overheat. We also wanted to be close to a bathtub we could fill with cold water to cool him down if it was necessary. We could tell right away this contraption was working and keeping Joey cool, doing the job we wanted it to do.

After a short time we even learned how to get around with little difficulty from the awkward design of the separate pieces with a short 5 or 6 foot hose connecting the pieces. Joey also adapted to this thing very quickly. I called Rhonda at ILC Dover and told her this splint was working better then we ever hoped and could they make a vest to do the same job. Rhonda told me that not only could they make a vest, they could make it so it would only be one piece that would be lighter than the splint and easier to use. The only drawback was it would take about 3 months to create this costume made equipment, but we could use the splint until his vest was ready. I then asked about how much all this was going to cost and was told to consider it a gift to Jocy. I'm not really sure they even realize everything this gift included, but by far the most important piece, was the gift of summer. Their equipment gave our son the ability to play outside in the summer heat with no adverse effects. By now I had been working in the O.R. for about six months and I was ready to begin taking emergency call. This was the one aspect of my new job I feared most because this is when my skills would really be put to the test. I think the thing that scared me most was the possibility of serious trauma, the kind that takes lives. I was afraid that if I wasn't good enough or fast enough I might cause someone to die. I also knew that this was a very real part of the job I had chosen for myself. My shift had also changed, I was now working the late shift from I 2:30pm to 9:00pm but having a job and some money in our pockets certainly was nice.

The first time I was on duty for emergency calls I learned that my personal fears were unfounded. It was a Friday night and I was still at work when our first emergency came in which was dealt with easily. By the time that case was finished another very serious emergency arrived, the kind of case I feared most. This case taught me that I could handle if the toughest of surgeries and helped lay my fears to rest.

Most of the doctors I worked with were very good at what they did and easy to work with. I also got stuck working with some surgeons that were very arrogant and obnoxious, these guys weren't fun to work with. I remembered something I learned from my grandfather who said" if it was always easy it wouldn't be called work", this was the kind of wisdom that at least offered some levity to the situation. I also knew from past experience that every job I ever did had at least one jerk that nobody wanted to work with and this job would be no exception.

Back at home Joey's behavior started to slip and he began hurting himself again. We didn't understand this because we had continued doing everything we were taught at the Kennedy Institute the year before. Margie called Susan in Baltimore to ask for advice, she was told that Kathy had left but thought we might be able to regain control with a few outpatient visits. We made an appointment and took him down to Baltimore. After some brief observations it was very apparent that this would of little help. Joey would need to return for inpatient care. Then the other shoe dropped and we were then told by Dr. Hyman that she too was moving on. Susan told us that she was beginning to burn out by the work she had been doing. We understood this completely but still did not want to give up this ally who had been so helpful in the past.

When we got home we called Joey's pediatrician and explained what we were told and asked him to start the paperwork to get the out of state approval from medicaid. I had private insurance through my employer, but from experience I knew to check to see how much of this next admission would be covered. We also knew that the medicaid Joey received would cover any portion of a medical bill that our private insurance didn't cover, provided the services were pre-approved. Our personal experiences of the past made us leave no stone unturned with respect to the expensive admission we were facing once again.

Joey was put on the Kennedy Institute's waiting list and could not be admitted until early the following year, 1990. Margie and I already knew that Joey would be given the best care we could ever want, but we still didn't want our son so far away again. We also knew if we wanted to overcome these behavior problems we had no other choice.

We were approached by our local News Paper, The Courier Post, to do a story about Joey and the rareness of his disease. The reporter, a gentleman named Jeffery wrote a very good in-depth article about Jeffery. He had a new's photographer come to the apartment to take pictures of Joey and our family. When Jeffery's story was published it made the front page and the piece he did was very well written and gave very accurate details. The article was so well written that it even brought tears to my eyes and I was one of the people interviewed for the information it contained. Jim also gave us the phone number to his desk and told us if we ever needed the assistance a news paper could provide, telling us not to hesitate to call if he could be helpful in any way. We had no idea how valuable his offer would become, nor did we know that Jeffery would be added to our growing list of allies.

Our fight to help Joey would begin to change, it was no longer a just war against the invisible threat that was trying to take our youngest sons life. We would also be forced to learn how to fight a bureaucracy that should have been there to help, who instead caused more problems then it solved.

Chapter 4

Late September 1989 was here and Margie and I were doing our level best to manage Joey's behavior along with Mark's needs, which to say the least was a very complicated task. We were both working hard to make ends meet and both of us felt like we were living in a pressure cooker. Then without warning another catastrophe strikes.

Margie had a day off and she got our sitter to watch Joey for an hour or two so she could take Mark shopping with one of his friends. Unfortunately while waiting to make a left into the parking lot of the store, she was hit from behind and pushed into the crowded on coming traffic and hit again head-on. Evidently this happened just before I left work to head home, for whatever reason I stopped by my mother's house on my way home. I had just pulled into her driveway a my mother came outside and told me Margie had been involved in a bad accident and she was at the Kennedy Hospital. I left immediately to go to the hospital feeling like my world was spinning out of control. Maybe it was the events of the early part of the year with the lose of my wife's father and sister only two days apart followed closely by Joey getting a bad pneumonia that caused me fear unlike anything I ever experienced before. When I got to the hospital I didn't want to go in because of what I might find, but somehow I found the courage to go in. Once in the emergency room I found my wife and she did not sustain any life threatening injuries, but she was badly banged up.

Margie's trauma included a serious Brain Concussion along with some neck, back and knee injuries. After a few hour's she was treated and released with instructions to follow up with our family doctor and specialists for her fresh injuries. I remember thanking God for sparing my wife, she had some problems we would have to deal but she was alive. At the time we had no clue what kind of problems she would have, but we knew that whatever they were we could overcome them.

Like a weird twist in an already sick nightmare we were now seeing doctor's regularly for both Joey and Margie. As fate would have it Margie's concussion left her with a very serious brain injury and the injuries to her back and neck left her with chipped and bulging disks, she also blew her right knee which would require surgery. I choose an Orthopedic surgeon I worked with frequently to care for her knee and do the necessary surgery, his name was Dr. Tom Obade. I knew from working with Dr. Obade that he was a very talented and skilled surgeon, but I also knew he was about as arrogant and obnoxious as they come. Dr. Obade put my wife on the surgical schedule for Monday of the following week and explained what he would do and that she would be inpatient for three days. I now had a new problem, I had to work and I had to care for both children, one of which was a handful that made it very hard to fmd a sitter. We somehow managed to find a girl that was very caring and loved kids, we also found she was a fast learner who was almost fearless with Joey's needs.

Monday came quickly and I took Margie to work with me so she could be admitted and prepped for her surgery early that afternoon. I was able to make arrangements with my supervisor to be with my wife until she was anaesthetized and sleeping. During her operation I did two very minor surgeries that were short in duration. I knew Margie was have an Arthroscopic procedure that was very safe, but I still worried like she was having Open Heart surgery. The staff! worked with kept me informed of her progress and offered me all the support I could ever want, I was lucky to work with people that caried about each other as much as these people did.

I was just finishing up the second surgery when Dr. Obade came into the Operating Room I was working in and told me her surgery was done. The doctor told me when I finished to come see him in our lounge so he could tell me what he found and did. Once in the lounge Dr. Obade told me she had tom some cartilage that we knew about from the MRI, he cleaned up her knee and put her leg in a Continuous Passive Motion Device or CPMD (a machine that constantly flexes and extends the leg with no patient effort). The doctor showed me the pictures of her knee joint and also told me that he injected her knee with Marcaine (a local anaesthetic like Novocaine that lasts up to 12 hours).

I went to the recovery room to see my wife who was still sleeping comfortably and stayed with her until she woke up. Once in her room I made sure she had everything she needed before I went home to attend to our children. The next day at work I checked on Margie every time I got a break, I even skipped lunch that day to be with her. By now she was very sore and was learning to hate that CPMD machine. During the afternoon a Physical Therapist came and took the machine off and started therapy. Now my poor wife didn't know which she hated more, the machine or the therapist, who was making her exercise her freshly repaired knee. When I went to spend some time with her after work I explained that as much as she didn't like what was happening because of the pain it caused, in the end she would be better off and walking without crutches much sooner. This really didn't help much at the time, but she tried to understand what I was telling her because she knew how much I cared about her.

After Margie was discharged we began to clearly see how profound the injury to her brain was, her short term memory was almost none existent. When her knee healed enough for her to start trying to tackle her normal activities the short term memory problem became very evident. On a Saturday she went to the grocery store less than a mile form home to get a few things and get out for a few minutes. About an hour later I received a collect call from my wife who was crying that she couldn't figure how to get home. I somehow calmed her down and gave her directions to get home. Once she got home we called her doctor and told him about this experience who made sure to notify her Neurologist of this problem. The Neurologist ordered an MRI and a BEG to be done on Monday and made an appointment to see her late the next day on Tuesday, so I could be with her.

Monday came and her Uncle Joe took her for the tests and she came home with her MRI films to take to the doctor. On Tuesday I took her to the Neurologist who after reading the films and the BEG report that he had to call for to get the results, gave us a diagnosis. The doctor told us Margie had a Post Concussion Syndrome, he explained that this was not uncommon following severe concussion but he told us that the only treatment available was therapy. He also told us that sometimes this can resolve itself and some people have to learn to live with it, which is what the therapy was designed to do. He gave her a prescription for the therapy and told us were she would need to go to receive the treatment.

Margie made an appointment for later that week and arranged a ride to the Therapist's office. When I got home she told me about her experience while crying because she felt like she was losing her mind. I got her calmed down and assured her that she could overcome this problem and I would help her anyway I possibly could.

The following week she started going to therapy three days a week, she learned how to compensate for her memory loss quickly. After only two weeks she was ready to try to drive herself to therapy following the directions she wrote. Margie also learned to write everything down and began to carry a small note book everywhere she went. The treatment she received was designed primarily to help people who suffered a stroke, it helped my precious wife learn to live with this problem very quickly and I was very proud of her accomplishments.

By now Thanksgiving was only a week away and something happened. I had just left the apartment to go to work, as I got in the car I had a problem with the door. This was a problem that popped up frequently and took no more then five minutes to fix, but I couldn't. I still don't fully understand what happened, but I just sat there crying, feeling like my world was spinning completely out of control. I managed to get back into our apartment and went straight into our bedroom and really lost it. Margie heard me come back in and found me sitting on the bed crying that I just wanted to go home which made no sense, even too me because I was home. I don't remember much before she took me to the Crisis Center. Once there with the help of some medication they were able to calm me down, after some counseling and a promise from me that I would not hurt myself and I would return for more counseling we were sent home.

My life was changing in ways I could not understand, I thought I was doing a good job of adapting and overcoming all of our problems of the past. I was being a man the way I was taught as a child, I thought everything was going good. I wasn't being faced with anything new or anything I haven't already survived, but for some reason I suddenly felt weak and out of control.

I returned for counseling and began a completely new education. The first thing I learned was that as hard as I tried to be strong, I was still human. The counselor I talked too told me she was surprised I lasted this long without help. She told me that we had been living through one crisis after another for 2 lh years and I never had any method of unloading the emotional baggage I was accumulating. She was right, I got very good at bottling up my emotions and hiding my worries and fears, unfortunately this bottle had it's own limit and finally broke. I still don't know why such a small problem suddenly ballooned into what I was now feeling. I was told to take the week off from work and they would try to find some private counseling for me. It turns out that the Crisis Center offered me counseling as more of a courtesy because of my circumstances, they were only suppose to offer crisis intervention mainly for suicide attempts.

I returned to work a week later and was called into the supervisor's office. Mary my supervisor told me she saw this coming but did not know how to intervene and did not want to butt-in where she didn't feel she belonged. Mary made sure I knew she would support anything I needed to do, to take care of my emotional health and stability. A week or two later my mother called to give me some information about a facility that she heard about on the radio. She told me about this outpatient program in NE Philadelphia that was created to treat depression and gave me a phone number for more information. I called and made an appointment to be evaluated for their program, I was scheduled for an appointment two weeks later.

I went to Philly for my appointment as scheduled, but this would be my first experience with a Psychiatric Hospital. As I drove my imagination ran wild, I had no idea what to expect when I got there. Friends Hospital was a very nice place, it was a very old facility that had been kept in pristine condition. The grounds were landscaped and manicured beautifully, and the buildings were equally beautiful inside and out. I think I half expected to find something from the movie "One Flew Over the Cuckoo's Nest" where I would meet people like Nurse Ratchet. As you can well imagine, I was dead wrong and most of my anxiety caused just by being there quickly evaporated.

I was evaluated by a Dr. Hand who was a very nice gentleman and the evaluation only lasted about an hour. When we finished the doctor thought I was a very appropriate candidate for their outpatient program. I was told that the program was five days a week and started a 9am until3pm and ifI wanted to attend, I would be able to start the first week of the approaching New Year. I was also told that all of this depended on approval by my health insurance coverage and my own willingness to see it through.

The next day Dr. Hand called and told me that my insurance did not cover outpatient mental health therapy, but they would cover inpatient care 100%. I remember thinking the insurance company must be crazier than me because they were willing to spend almost three time the cost of outpatient care (and we wonder why health insurance is having the problems they now have- well da). Upon hearing this I wouldn't agree to anything without more information and made an appointment to go back to find out what I would be getting myself into.

I went back to meet with Dr. Hand again to get the information I needed to make an intelligent decision for myself. I learned that I could basically come and go as I pleased and if I absolutely hated it there I could sign myself out in 72 hours after requesting to be discharged. I was shown the building I would be staying in and a patient room like I would have. This place was nice, I would have a private room with a shared bathroom like everyone else. I was introduced to the staff that was currently on duty who seemed like very good people who liked what they did. I even met and talked to some of the patients and found they were all everyday people that were having tough time, in many ways just like me.

After this meeting and a tour with Dr. Hand I agreed to treatment in their hospital, with the understanding I would be discharged in time to take Joey back to Baltimore to start his treatment on February 5, 1990. I was given a tentative admission date of January 7, I signed some papers to get the insurance process started and left to bring all this information home to Margie. I made arrangements at work for a medical leave of absence and tried to focus on the Christmas Holiday that was now on my heels.

Thanksgiving came and went that year almost without notice and I wanted to make the best of Christmas. I had a job this year and was able to give better gifts and I know that's not what Christmas is about, but it still feels good to give people you love things they want, rather than need. Our family had a very enjoyable Holiday despite everything that was happening. As the New Year arrived so did my second thoughts, I kept asking ifl was making a mistake. I knew I didn't want to fall apart like I did just a few short weeks ago. I also didn't like feeling weak, I decided with the help of my wife that if this would help me regain my emotional strength, I was making the right choice.

I took my wife over to the hospital where I would be staying so she could write directions and find landmarks so she come to visit me and get home without problems. I had her drive over with me to make sure her directions were accurate so I wouldn't worry about her making the trip. Margie found her way like a pro and I knew she would be okay.

January 7, 1990 Mark Jr is 7, Joey is 4 and I think I must really be crazy to go through with this admission. Margie and I left to get too Friends Hospital by 10 o'clock that morning. This was the first time Margie had actually been inside this hospital and she commented about the antique beauty of the place. After signing the admission papers and meeting with the doctor we were taken to my room to unpack. About 1 o'clock Margie and I went to the cafeteria to have lunch together, afterwards she went home. The biggest problem I was having with this whole thing was the fact that I was the one that needed help and it felt so awkward. I always felt like I was the one that was supposed to do the helping. I look back at life now and I am amazed at how destiny or whatever it is, can turn the tables anytime it damn well pleases.

My first day at Friends wasn't easy, I did want to be away from home and leave Margie with both kids by herself By the second day I was feeling better about what I was doing, I met other patients and quickly made friends. I learned that the most beneficial therapy was just talking to the other people that were all there for the same reason, but with different circumstances. I was told by my doctor that the intended effect of their social environment. After a few days and being at ease with the staff! began to call Friends Hospital; Toon Town, not out of disrespect but for the stigma that comes with being in a Psychiatric Hospital. Surprisingly the nickname I was using caught on and was even being used by the sta~ but only under appropriate circumstances.

By the end of the first week I knew I made the right choice, I was given choices for the therapies I needed. The rules were very reasonable and easy to follow and everybody there treated everyone else with respect and dignity. Margie was coming to visit with me daily and after a few days she remarked that she could see me improving. My stay in Toon Town was more like going on a retreat than being in a hospital and I knew this was probably the single best thing I ever did for myself. I stayed for two weeks and when I came home I felt like a new man.

During my treatment at Friends Hospital I learned my biggest problem was denial. I refused to believe that Joey's condition would last throughout his life and he wouldn't just outgrow it. I also found that working in a main Operating Room was probably not my best choice for work because we dealt with tragedy on a daily basis. I had to deal with too many emergencies at home to work a job that only added to the stress. I also had time to make some rational decisions, which included finding a job at a outpatient surgical center. All of this made returning home where life must go on an easier task and helped me find the strength to deal with our ongoing problems. I also had a counselor near home that I could use to unload my ugly baggage that was also affordable, only $5.00 per session. I had been given the emotional tools I would need to continue living in the pressure cooker we called home.

Once home it was time to pick up where I had left off and begin taking care of my responsibilities. Margie had an appointment for chronic pain management at the Summit Surgical Center to get treatment for her back and neck injuries. While I waited I filled out an application for employment, half expecting it to hit the circular file when I left. I got the shock of my life, the OR Supervisor gave me an interview on the spot. During the interview I told the supervisor named Bissy about my situation at home, she told me she had seen the story on the news and in the paper. I told her about my very recent hospitalization, which she understood and commended me for doing. I also explained about Joey's upcoming admission in Baltimore, that ifi was hired I could only work part time until our son was discharged.

Bissy offered me a job and asked when I could start. I explained that I had not yet returned to my current job and I would be returning on February 141 \ pending written medical clearance. I told Bissythat I would like to give at least two weeks notice before leaving Underwood Memorial. I gave a tentative start date ofMarch, 7th, I also said if something changed that allowed me to start sooner I would call. Upon hearing this I was welcomed aboard and offered a tour of the facility. During the tour I met some of the staff and I was very impressed by the layout of the Operating rooms. Before leaving I got Bissy's phone number and promised to call if anything changed and that I would call the week before I was supposed start.

In only two short weeks we would be taking Joey to Baltimore for another round of treatment that once again included parent training two days a week. We had a problem, we still had not gotten our out of state treatment authorization from NJ Medicaid and the request was made six months ago. Feeling ready to take on this challenge I called our medicaid office and asked if we were going to receive the necessary authorization for Joey's impending admission. I was told no decision had been made yet and we would get an answer before the admission date. I knew from experience that fighting with these people only made things worse so I thanked the girl and agreed to wait, even though I knew I could not trust the state of New Jersey to do the right thing.

Friday 2, 1990 we got a phone call from the Kennedy Institute admissions department and was informed that they had not yet received the authorization from NJ Medicaid and if they didn't have it by the end of the business day at 6 o'clock, Joey's admission would be postponed. I finally got the mail and the admission was being denied for a lack of information. I called the phone number listed on the letter of denial, now I was livid being denied on the last business day before the admission date. I demanded to speak to the doctor that made the decision and was told he was in a meeting and he would call back. I waited another hour and tried calling again, I was given a different excuse with another promise to return my call. I knew this Dr. Bell was putting me off so I told the secretary that if he did not return my call within a half hour he would hear from the Courier Post. When I hung up I was hoping Jeff meant what he said when he made the offer to help in any way. I had just made a threat that without Jeff would have been empty.

I called Jeff at the number he provided and was surprised that he was there (the paper keeps him very busy). After all the pleasantries of not having spoke to each other for a few months, I explained the problem. Jeff got some information and Dr. Bell's phone number and promised to call me back. By now it was 3 o'clock in the afternoon and I was pacing the floor trying to find another idea when the phone rang.

Dr. Bell finally called and wanted to know why I had called the Courier Post ? I countered with a flurry of answers that would have made the most seasoned lawyer proud. I told him first that it was too bad for him that Freedom of the Press is a right and I resented the fact that he even questioned my using it for my child. I then told him if he actually knew anything about medicine, he would know by all the x-ray reports to rule out skull fractures, :facial bone fractures and positive reports of repeated nose fractures, the admission was necessary. I went further and promised that if my son sustained a permanent injury or worse from this day forth, that I would do everything possible to have him prosecuted like the criminal he was. I told him that he had only two and a half hours to do whatever it took it approve Joey's admission or face the consequences. Dr. Bell now had his back to the wall and it felt good to be able to holding him there.

I called Jeff and told him about Dr. Bell's call. I told him I don't know how he did it but Dr. Bell said Joey would be approved before the dead line. Jeff's reply was that he made it clear, that this story would be on the cover of the next days Courier Post and how that type of honest and provable PR can end a career. Jeff was true to his word and came through for Joey in a big way and I came away a proud father who was only doing his job and nothing more. Around 5:30 that evening we received a call from the admission's department at the Kennedy Institute to inform us they just got the last of the paperwork via fax and Joey's admission had been approved. Jeff was added to our ever growing list of allies and I fully understood the term of "the power of the press".

During Joey's final weekend home before going back to Baltimore for an unspecified amount of time we did everything we could to make our time last. Being February and the coldest part of our winter our activities were limited, but we still found things to enjoy with both boys. Margie and I packed everything Joey would need and then we packed for ourselves. Neither of us wanted this chore or the ordeal we now knew to expect. It just didn't seem fair that we had no choices or alternatives, it was Baltimore or nothing and that sucked.

Monday morning came and we took Joey back to be admitted in the Kennedy Institute and we hoped it would be the last admission there. This was his second stay in Baltimore, so we had a good idea what to expect and we still knew that Joey would get the best care available in the world. From a parents perspective none of that matters, we wanted our children home where they get love and not just treatment. In many ways this trip would be different, most noticeably was the absence of Susan Hyman and Kathy who we had grown to trust. We still kept in touch with Susan who now worked at the University of Maryland in downtown Baltimore.

Margie and I met the new Behaviorist a young lady named Lynn, she was very nice and seemed to be at least as competent as Kathy was. This behaviorist had many of the qualities as Dr. Hyman, she was a hard worker and set goals for herself that were unattainable. Lynn was very intelligent with all the compassion of a saint, she was honest and would listen to our concerns. Just like Susan she made sure we understood what she was telling us, answering our questions carefully and honestly. After we answered the questions that now seemed like the history of the world, Margie and I left to check into our room down the street and get some lunch. The hotel was now called the Johns Hopkins Inn and offered a substantial discount for families of patients in Johns Hopkins Medical Center. This time I was working and was better prepared for the expenses, but Murphies Law said it would not be nearly as expensive, just because we could better afford the trips back and forth. The admission process lasted three days again, but this time my wife and I took advantage of the entertainment Baltimore had to offer. Joey was now 4 years old and was not as easy to distract when it was time to leave everyday. During the second day we learned that because this stay was for Behavior Modification only our son would be checked out daily by doctors that would rotate monthly. This information made his mother and I a little bit uncomfortable, but we knew this was the best medicine in the world we could find.

The three days went by quickly and it was time to leave. Joey made it hard, he knew what was happening and hung onto his mother and me for dear life. Now he was old enough to know we were about to leave and he understood what he heard. Our son made it very obvious that he didn't like what we were doing. Margie and I finally left with tears in our eyes and questions in our heart. On the ride home we kept asking each other if we were doing the right thing and the answer was just as mixed up as we were. Logically we already knew this wasn't just the right thing to do, it was the only thing to do. Unfortunately a parents heart is not nearly as decisive and our hearts told us that Joey needed this treatment, but at the same time it said we wanted what he needed at home. We finally came to the conclusion that it was the right choice, that it just felt wrong.

When we got back to New Jersey, we picked Mark up at his grandmothers. My mother asked how was Joey? We explained about the problem we had leaving and how we wished he didn't have to be so far from home again. We also told her that this time there was no real medical component attached to this admission other than his daily medical requirements. My mother knew we weren't happy and we knew she was concerned.

Two years ago we were in the same place doing the same thing, now we had to do it all over again, with the exception of medical tests. Margie and I drew solace from the fact that the last time around we saw so much improvement in Joey that it made the ordeal so worthwhile. We hoped that would be the case this time, but with our crystal ball broken we had no way of knowing what the result would be. I had one thing going for me I didn't have before, I would be seeing a counselor to help keep me from over filling my emotional bottle again.

The next night I went for my intake appointment to get my counseling started. I answered all the questions and signed all the papers and met my counselor, her name was Susan too. I made an appointment for my first real private session for the following week. I knew I needed this, but I worried about the emotional health of my oldest son and my wife. They had been seeing everything I saw and were doing almost everything I had done, so I asked about counseling for them. I wanted to help the people I love most in the world to avoid the emotional breakdown I had already experienced.

When I got home I told Margie that I was going to arrange for her and Mark to get some counseling and by her response you might think I just killed her best friend. Margie was adamantly opposed to seeing someone, saying she didn 't need it. I explained my concerns to her and thought that even if we did family counseling it couldn't hurt. Margie was still opposed until I mentioned how all this had to be having a negative effect on little Mark. After all, he was young and highly impressionable and seeing his little brother get so much unavoidable attention, he must have felt left out at least on some level Neither of us felt like our family was in trouble and I wanted to prevent whatever problems we could. This was something that no one could argue with, so she agreed to going as a family for the sake of prevention.

The rest of the week was quiet and frighteningly uneventful. We called to check on Joey every morning and evening, we worried about him constantly. That weekend we took Mark to Baltimore to visit Joey and we were pleased to find him playing happily. As soon as Joey saw us he dropped his toys and came running to us smiling from ear to ear. In some ways that was a joyful moment, his mother and I also knew that it meant he missed us and because of the circumstances that was very painful. Speaking for myself! think it would have been easier to be getting shot at on the front line of a war somewhere. I had learned the hard way how deep emotional scars ran and how the pain that created them never really goes away.

We spent the day playing with the kids and enjoying our time together, which was now bittersweet, again because of circumstances we learned to hate. At the end of the day we tore ourselves away to go home and again Joey didn't want us to leave without him. We could see the effect this had on Mark, which reenforced the idea of counseling. On Sunday a friend of mine came over and he watched the Eagles football game with Mark and I. Margie spent the day with one of her friends shopping at the local mall. Sunday night came and my wife and I packed for our overnight stay back in Baltimore. We sat and told Mark we were sorry we had to leave him with his grandmother again. He told us not to worry about him saying we would only be gone overnight and Joey is the one stuck down there. Mark was being forced to grow up too fast and while he made me proud of his maturity, I also worried about that too, a 7 year old boy shouldn't have to think like that. I was looking forward to my first session with my new shrink more and more each day.

Monday morning we dropped Mark off at school were he would be picked up in the afternoon by my mother and left to be with Joey. After checking into our room we went to the unit and again Joey was thrilled to see us. When we started working with him I had forgotten how hard some of the things we would be asked to do was. This time around Joey's behavior was much more violently self abusive. The things he did to himself seemed so evil almost like Satan himself was in control. During the sessions whenever Joey would start to hurt himself everything was stopped and he was very well protected. I knew they would not allow him to cause himself any serious injury but that didn't make what we were doing any easier.

By the time we took a break for lunch I was feeling totally beat down, like I was fighting an advisory that could not be beaten. During the second half of the day I had to stop and get away, I sat on the floor in a corner crying. One of the unit nurses came to my aid and I couldn't even talk. I felt like I was being forced to hurt my boy in way I could never dream of. Now the sessions were being interrupted because of my weakness. A few minutes later Joey was back on the unit playing with his aid. Lynn and Margie came and got me, my wife held me and Lynn said we should take a walk for a few minutes to give me a chance to clear my head. She told us when we came back she wanted to talk with me.

Margie and I went outside and I smoked a few cigarettes and got myself together to go back. Once back at the unit Lynn took me to her office to talk, she told me that what I was feeling was normal. She explained that she would worry more about any parent that could do what we were doing, without becoming emotional. Lynn told me that what we were doing was one of the toughest things a parent could be asked to do. I told Lynn that I understood all this and knew this was all necessary for Joey's well-being and how understanding still did not make it tolerable. This was such a mixed bag of emotions that the concept of right and wrong seemed to be missing within the mix.

Logically I knew beyond any doubt that this was the right thing for Joey, neither Marge or me wanted him to hurt himself the way he was. My heart said that doing things with him to make him hurt himself was wrong and the worse part was that none of us knew what the trigger was that started the self injury. All we were really doing was normal stuff, we would play with him and then make him put the toys away. We would show him how to do things and ask him to copy what we did and for whatever reason, Joey would just go off and start to hurt himself. To me this all defied logic because we weren't doing anything that should have made him angry.

After our short discussion Lynn and I found Margie playing with Joey and called it a day. Lynn suggested we do something that was fun and to enjoy ourselves that evening. This lady knew Margie and I had already taken quite a beating by life and we had way too many years ahead of us to burn out now.

My wife and I went out for a romantic dinner at a restaurant overlooking the Baltimore Harbor and then did some shopping in a mall at the Inner Harbor. We had an enjoyable evening despite the reason for our being there. I would have given anything just to make all this unnecessary but there was no magic that could make that happen.

The next day working with Joey was pretty much the same, we experienced tantrums for no apparent reason and we kept doing what we were told. Before we left for home we had a meeting with Lynn who wanted to share some ideas and goals. Lynn said that Joey was functional enough to be toilet trained and would like our permission to try. Margie and I were never happy about the fact that we were unable to train him and get him out of diapers so we gave her our blessing to try. Lynn also wanted to try to teach Joey how to use a fork and spoon better when he ate and eliminate his need to use his fingers. She thought that if he was taught to use an adaptive plate called a palette along with adaptive utensils he should learn how to use them quickly. Lynn asked us to get some training pants for Joey so she could start the toilet training as soon as possible.

As Margie and I drove home we talked about what was going on. We were both thrilled about the prospect of :finally getting Joey out of diapers and hoped Lynn would be successful We also liked the idea of Joey being able to use utensils to eat more appropriately. My wife and I liked Lynn and felt she knew what she was doing and we were also comfortable with her being Joey's advocate in our absence. Needless to say we still weren't happy about Joey's need to be there.

Once we got home and picked Mark up, it was time to keep moving forward. I was looking forward to returning to work the next day after being out for six weeks. I was however a little worried about the stigma of spending time in a Psychiatric Hospital, which I quickly learned was unfounded.

My first day at work was like I never left with the exception that all my coworkers asked how I was doing. They all seemed genuinely concerned about me and my family and assured me that they thought I made a wise choice for myself My boss was happy to see me doing so well and asked if I was getting follow-up care, which I assured her I was. I then dropped my bombshell an gave my two weeks notice. Mary told me that in light of my situation, doing less serious outpatient surgeries was probably a good idea and said she was sorry to see me go. I thanked Mary for giving me the opportunity to refresh my skills and that it was a valuable learning experience that I would never forget. Mary then dropped a bombshell of her own, she told me I was on-call that weekend. When I got home that evening I asked Margie how Joey was doing when she called to check on him. I also told her that I was on-call over the weekend so she knew visiting Joey on Saturday was not possible.

My weekend emergency call was a shift from hell. I was required to be in from 8:00am until 4:30pm both Saturday and Sunday and be ready to return through the night both nights until 6:00am on Monday. I went to work Saturday morning and my call partner Joanne and I found things to do, we stocked all the rooms with whatever they needed and tried to find busy work to help pass the time.

Shortly after 2pm we had our first emergency surgery and then it was like the damn burst with one after another. In all we did 7 emergency surgeries, we got a few short breaks that we used to rest before the rush ended. I called home between cases a few times to check up on my family and told Margie that I would need her to pack for me for Mondays trip. I finally got home about 2:30am Monday morning and promptly fell asleep for a few short hours before leaving for Baltimore later that morning.

On our way out we had to stop at Underwood Memorial Hospital so I could drop off the pager for whoever was on-call that night. After which we went back to Baltimore and I felt too tired to face the work we needed to do with Joey, but it had to be done.

Once back at the Kennedy Institute we followed our normal routine of checking in to our room and running to the unit to see our son and start working. Lynn told us Joey had a very good week and was learning to use the adaptive utensils and pallette appropriately. She then looked at me and asked if I was okay. I told her about my weekend from hell at work and that

I just needed some sleep. Upon hearing this Lynn said she would try to go easy on us today and maybe even find a way to let me go back to our room to grab a nap. I told her I would like that but I didn't want to cause a loss of time that might keep Joey there even a minute longer then necessary.

After lunch that day we got a pleasant surprise, Dr. Susan Hyman came to visit with us. Margie and I gave her a hug a told her how much we wished she was still there. Susan told us that with our permission she would like to stop in for time to time to see Joey and check on things. We told her nothing would make us happier and how much we appreciated her concern for our son. Susan said that Joey was very special to her and she was happy to see him again and she only wished it could be under better circumstances. Margie and I couldn't have agreed more. We told Lynn that she could share any information they had with Dr. Hyman and asked for the release to make it legal. We knew that Dr. Hyman would not be providing any treatment personally, but we were willing to follow any advice she had to offer. This also helped Margie and I feel better about his stay down. there. We were getting to know Lynn enough to know she could be trusted to do whatever was in Joey's best interest. Now we had the best doctor we ever met, who we also considered a friend, wanting to check on our son. With our surprise visitor and lots of coffee a nap was no longer necessary, although I was glad I wasn't asked to make any major decisions that day because I doubt I would have been able to make intelligent choices.

This week was not much different then the week before except Joey had been fitted with a helmet to help protect him from himself. Joey didn't like the helmet and kept trying to take it off and he wasn't alone. Margie and I weren't thrilled about the helmet either, but we did like the protection it offered our son.

At dinner time we were asked to stay just to observe the eating protocol they were implementing with Joey. We were impressed how all the children on the unit (never more then eight) worked together to set the table and help get their food. The children that were able, carried their own trays and the others could not that would get their own beverage. Joey knew however that his drink came from the nurse who thickened it for him. Instead of going to the food cart he went to the door to the the nurses station, where he knew the nurse would promptly bring him his thickened drink. There was one nurse named Annie who was very creative about what she prepared for Joey to drink. Annie was trying to make sure

Joey got a variety of flavors so she would thicken juice, soda, milk and chocolate milk you name it and she would thicken it.

After the children finished their dinner they all helped with the clean up, each child that was able cleaned up his or her place setting. They even rotated daily for who would wash the table after their meal. This was something that they didn't do during Joey's first stay at the Kennedy Institute. Margie and I were impressed by the way the children knew what was expected of them. We were told that a child that didn't want to cooperate would get time out for a few minutes, which to a young child was a long time. Susan may not have worked here anymore but this was keeping with her idea; not to treat a disabled child like they are handicapped.

It seemed like every time we went down to Baltimore for parent training the time went by faster. Margie and I didn't like being there but we sure did like being with our son and for that reason we could never be there long enough. Our two days flew by and it was time to leave Joey and go home. By now Joey was getting used to the idea that mom and dad had to leave and he would give us our hugs and kisses and then go about his business. This was making it much easier for us to leave. This week would be my last few days working at Underwood before starting my new job at the Summit Surgical Center the following week. On Friday, on my last day my, coworkers threw me a going away party, which reinforced my opinion of these fine people. This was a group of good down to earth people and I told them that it had been a privilege to have worked with them and how I hoped we could somehow stay in touch with one another.

I started working at the Summit and fell right into my new position scrubbing for and assisting in outpatient surgical procedures. I started part time and worked three, ten hour days. I was surprised by the number of cases we would do, on average we did between 40 and 50 cases a day divided between the six operative suites we had. It was almost like a production line turnover, except that each patient was given very good individual care and attention, which gave the Summit Surgical Center a reputation that was beyond reproach.

In the beginning I was scrubbing so often that the skin on my arms would become raw. Like everything else I learned to adapt to this number of daily scrubs and learned how to protect my skin. I was also surprised by the team atmosphere we had, everybody helped everybody else, which would account for the number of cases we were able to do with competence and success. As the weeks went by Joey's behavior was beginning to be understood and the behavior modification protocols implemented would begin to work. This time around his behavior patterns were not as easily understood as the last time he was here. The reasons for his self-injurious behavior was much more complex, but the modification techniques were still simple and easy to follow. During this time Margie received a call from her pastor and learned that the Lutheran Brotherhood was having a back to the Phillies night for Joey in about three weeks at Veterans Stadium in Philadelphia. The pastor told her that this was arranged with the hope that the Phillies Baseball Team Charity might be able to help Joey in some way. He told Margie he would drop off six tickets for VIP seating and parking at our apartment and he hoped we could make it. He also promised to get their prayer group to start praying for Joey and strength for the rest of the family, he then prayed with Margie before hanging up. Margie and I new Joey would not be able to go to the game, but we planned on going because we were willing to accept any help that might be available. We also knew that Mark would really love going to the game.

The Easter Holiday came and went almost without notice. On Easter Sunday some of the family came to Baltimore to visit with Joey and we all had dinner at a nearby restaurant, which helped make it feel more like the Easter Holiday we grew up with. We all had a very enjoyable day along with a good meal but it still was not the same as home.

The weeks began to go fast, with each new week going by quicker then the week before. The strangest thing was that while each day at home or at work seemed to drag on forever, but as I looked back at the day it almost seemed like it flew by in a blur. The most important aspect of the time was Joey and now he was making real progress. Margie and I hoped he would be coming home soon and being able to put this necessary stay behind us. However Joey's still undiagnosed disease would soon remind us that our son's life was still fragile and try yet again to cut his precious life tragically short.

Chapter 5

Joey's stay at the Kennedy Institute was beginning to go fast, with each new week seeming to go by faster then the week before. Then two weeks after Easter our sons disease reared it ugly head to make the nightmare we were already living, even worse. Joey got a very severe aspiration pneumonia due to primary aspiration (remember in chapter 1, food inhaled directly into the lungs). It was a Monday morning, before leaving for another round of parent training when Margie called and talked to one of the unit nurses to check on Joey. The nurse said Joey had just been seen by the doctor and was just fine. After the call we left for Baltimore and during our drive Margie kept saying that she just had a bad feeling that something was wrong. I told her it was probably just a mothers anxiety and to try to stop worrying that she had just called and Joey is fine. Upon arrival we checked into our room and went over to the unit expecting to see our boy, but he wasn't there. Lynn told us that about an hour ago Joey didn't look too good and had a nurse check him out, which she did. After the nurses assessment, Joey was found to be running a fever of 101 o and his lungs were congested.

The doctor was called and Joey was taken to the hospital next door, where he was admitted to the Pediatric Intensive Care Unit (P.I.C.U.). When Margie and I arrived at the P.I.C.U. (called picku) to be with Joey, but we were kept out do to our son was having his first Grand Maul Seizure. Margie wasn't happy and went to his bed despite the nurses attempt to keep us out so we would not interfere with their treatment of this crisis. Joey's seizure was finally controlled with medication after an eternity of about fifteen minutes. With the crisis over the doctor explained about the pneumonia and the cause, he also explained that a Pulrnonologist had been called to help treat this illness.

Joey's stay for Behavior Modification had now turned into a medical nightmare that would put his already fragile life at risk once again. Margie and I had a another problem too, we were afraid to leave him alone more then 100 miles from home while facing this crisis, so we would have find away to change our plans. We had a little more then 24 hours to find a solution and started with a hospital Social Worker. The Social Worker was able to provide financial help for our room and meals to extend our stay, but we still had other problems to work out. I just started a new job, so I did not want to call out and Mark Jr needed his parents, plus the back to the Phillies game was the coming Saturday. We decided that we would somehow find away to make it happen, or at least do our very best trying.

The Pulrnonologist saw Joey along with the X-rays and lab results so he could find the best treatment plan and answer our questions. When this doctor finished his evaluation he explained how he planed to treat this pneumonia. He told Margie and I that Joey would survive but the repeated insults to his lungs was becoming irreversible and our son would eventually need to be put on a respirator if the insults were not stopped. The doctor told us Joey would need a Gastrostomy Tube again and another set of studies with the Dysphagia Specialist to see what if anything Joey could safely consume by mouth. The Pulrnonologist also said that with our consent, the Gastrostomy should be done as soon as possible and he would call a General Surgeon to see Joey and get him on the schedule for surgery.

Margie and I knew what all this meant from our experience two years prior and we weren't thrilled by the prospect of that damn tube. We also knew if we did not consent Joey's life would be cut tragically short and he would end up suffocating to death. We looked at each other and said remember no regrets knowing only to well that the wrong decision would leave nothing but regrets. After only a few minutes Margie and I knew what the answer had to be and we unhappily gave our consent. I told the doctor I had only one request and asked him to call a surgeon he would pick for his own child, with a knowing smile he promised he would get our son the best.

Joey was now fast asleep from the medication used to break the seizure, so Margie and I went back to the unit to talk to Lynn and try to find out what happened. Lynn told us she was working with Joey who was being cooperative and happy. In a matter of minutes he suddenly looked bad, so she got a nurse to evaluate him. She said she had never seen anybody get that sick that quickly, which in a weird way finally validated what only

Margie and I had witnessed before. We explained what the doctor told us and with any luck Joey would be back the following week.

We went back to the P.I.C.U. to be with our son only to find him still sleeping and that visiting hours did not permit us to see him for another hour. The visiting hours were quite strange to us, we were only allowed to see him for fifteen minutes every two hours from 8am till 8pm. While waiting we got some good news which was Joey's oxygen levels in his blood had improved dramatically and if he kept improving he would be in a regular patient room the following day.

My wife and I had plenty of time to talk to try to figure out what our options were for the remainder of the week. We decided that I should call Bissy, my new boss to see if it was possible for me to take an extra day off because of the situation? If I could then I would stay until Wednesday and Margie would stay thru the weekend with Joey. I called Bissy to explain the situation and was told that the extra day off would not be a problem because of a very lite schedule throughout the week. I then called my mother and asked if she could watch Mark until Wednesday and explained what was going on, this was not a problem either. After two short calls we had most of the lose ends tied up and a new plan was now in place.

By the time we were allowed to see Joey again we was still sleeping and we just stood there both holding the same hand because of the IV in the other arm. The nurse was kind enough not to chase us out after the allowed fifteen minutes were up, but she did ask us not to stay too much longer. Margie and I stayed about a half hour and left before getting the nurse in trouble. During the hour and a half we had to wait before seeing our son again, so we ran out to a small variety store to try to find some toys for Joey to help him pass the time. We also went back to our room for a few minutes to relax and grab a much needed break. Like everything else that is enjoyable it just did not last long enough and before we knew it, the time that we could be with our son again was here. Unfortunately time is a commodity that we felt we could not afford to waste, because of the value we got from our time with Joey.

Back at the hospital Joey was finally waking up and he reached out to his mother and I for a hug, this was a request we were only too happy to acknowledge and we gave him the hugs he wanted. We knew only too well that emotional support for Joey was always a key element in his survival and it was his fight that we could only support. We also knew that the kind of love that parents have for their children was the best weapon we could give Joey to win this fight.

I have learned throughout the years that when you are faced with time constraints, there is never enough time and somehow the clock seems to go faster. Tuesday Joey was moved to a regular patient room where his mother and I could stay 24 hours a day. We also met with the surgeon who had scheduled Joey's surgery for the following day, hopefully by late morning. He explained that he was going to do a PEG (Percutaneous Endoscopic Gastrostomy) procedure and it should only take about a half hour including anesthesia time. I understood this from working in the operating room and scrubbing for this procedure at Underwood Memorial. I again had a request and asked the surgeon if he could either remove the old scare or go through the old scar just for aesthetic value. To this the surgeon was reluctant to make a promise other than he would try to make the outcome as aesthetically pleasing as possible.

I did my best to explain this stuff to Margie and told her that the procedure was about as safe as any surgery could be. I also understood that to a mother there is no such thing as a safe surgery when it being done to their child. I was just as worried as my wife, except I worried more about the anesthesia and it's impact on Joey's lungs. We stayed with Joey throughout the day until he finally fell asleep that night.

Wednesday morning came quickly and Joey's surgery was moved up, we arrived by 7am and he was prepped and ready to go by 9am. I was surprised to learn that one parent was allowed to accompany Joey into the operating room until he was asleep. Margie asked me if I minded going with him because I had a better understanding of what to expect, so I agreed.

Once in the operating room Joey was becoming understandably scared and I did my best to comfort him. As soon as he was on the table the Anaesthesiologist gave Joey the medicine that induced sleep and asked me to kiss him goodnight. I instead asked the Anesthesiologist to intubate Joey to protect his airway and start breathing for him and the doctor obliged my request. I knew that anesthesia is most dangerous during induction (putting a patient to sleep) and emergence (waking the patient), so I was partially content knowing he was well past the first hurdle. I however continued to worry along with my wife until he was in the recovery room and safe.

Only fifteen or twenty minutes passed before the surgeon came out and told us the surgery was done and our son was okay. We were told he would be in recovery for at least an hour so we went to get some coffee and discuss our plans for the rest of the week.

We decided that if there were no problems or complications with Joey, I would return Saturday morning with Mark Jr to visit Joey. We figured that if we left by mid afternoon we would be home in plenty of time for the game. I would then take Margie back Sunday morning and we would decide then if she would stay, this was the only part of the plan we left open because on Monday we would be returning anyway.

Joey was finally back in his room and other then being groggy from the anesthesia he looked good. He was also fighting hard to beat the pneumonia and doing a good job. I suppose every father wants their sons to be tough, but Joey was teaching me a different kind of toughness and pride. I had this little boy that loved everybody almost to a fault and he was forced to look death in the face in his four short years of life more then any adult I ever met, but without fear he always fought to win. I know if it were me I would have probably given up long ago, but Joey made me proud by the way he would fight with the intent of winning. I guess he just didn't know any different, after all he had been doing this for more then half of his young life. I do know that I thanked God everyday for giving my boy the will to survive and the strength he needed to win all the battles he had already faced.

I picked Mark up and as usual my mother asked I spent the rest of the day with Joey and finally left around dinner time to go home and get Mark. The drive home was uneventful except for the rush hour traffic and being alone. This helped to remind me how much I did not miss driving trucks for a living and how lonely the road can be, fortunately it was only a two hour drive.

I picked Mark up and as usual my mother asked how her other grandson was? I told her everything I knew, which is never enough and asked if she could get Mark after school if I needed her too? I told her that I hoped he would be able to stay with our friend Trish whose son was in school with Mark so he would be able to play and have some fun. Margie and I always worried about the effect all this was having on our oldest son, but we could only do our best.

Once home I called Margie to let her know I was home safe with Mark and fortunately I was able to make the arrangements with Irish to help with Mark as I had hoped. I hadn't eaten since lunchtime so I ordered a Pizza for Mark and me and spent the rest of the evening watching television with my oldest son until his bedtime. I got my stuff ready for work in the morning, called my wife again and laid in bed not able to sleep waiting for my alarm clock to ring.

In the morning I got Mark ready for school and left for work, I was looking forward to thinking about something else for ten hours. All my coworkers wanted to know how Joey was and did I need anything, they all wanted to help from the boss on down. Eventually the questions stopped and the mental break I was looking for came and I enjoyed having to think about my work, instead of my personal problems. The 2 days I worked that week went too fast and the weekend came quickly too. During this time a neighbor stopped by and introduced me to a friend of his, Billy who had been away for a while. Billy and I quickly became friends, so I offered him a ticket for the baseball game that Saturday night. I personally was looking forward to getting back to Baltimore to be with Joey and my wife. Now most guys would say I'm crazy but they were more important to me then any baseball game could ever be, besides I've never been much of a baseball fan.

Saturday morning Mark and I left for Johns Hopkins Medical Center early and surprised Joey and their mother. I was thrilled to see Joey doing so well so quickly and hoped he would be getting back to the Kennedy Institute soon. I realize it may sound selfiSh, but I wanted this admission behind us and Joey home where he belonged. Margie told me that Joey would begin getting feed via the tube for the first time on Sunday and if everything went well he would go back to the unit on Tuesday. The previous week was a nightmare, but now we were seeing some light at the end of this hellish week long tunnel. As planned we stayed until the afternoon and left for home so we would make the game in that evening.

Once home everybody that was going to the game met us at our apartment and I introduced my wife to Billy. We piled in the car and went to the game, looking forward to having some fun for a much needed change. This was actually the first time I went to a Major League Baseball game, until now I had never even been inside the Veterans Stadium We all had a great time and we wished Joey could have been there too, but that was just not possible. The Phillies team gave Mark and Joey an autographed pennant and Phillies hats, for a change Mark got a chance to feel special and he really had a great time. After the game we stopped at an Ice-cream Parlor to get Sundays before going home. We asked Billy if he wanted to take a ride with us the following day to meet Joey and after some hesitation he agreed.

During the ride to Baltimore we told Billy all about Joey and he admitted his concern about meeting our youngest son because he did know what to expect. We assured him he had nothing to worry about and told him that just seeing Joey he would never know he had the problems he had. When we arrived Mark Jr and Margie went in to see Joey (only two visitors per patient) and Billy and I waited in the solarium I was surprised when they came out with Joey and like all that came before Billy's fear just melted away. Joey has always been able to touch people in a way I can't even begin to explain and he did so again with our new friend. We were allowed to take Joey out for a while, so we went down to the Inner Harbor to walk around and give Joey some fresh air and sunshine. We had a great time watching the sidewalk acts people were doing. At the end of a very fast day we grudgingly took Joey back to the hospital and stayed with him until early evening before we came home.

Margie and I knew we would be back the next day so she came home too, but Joey carried on and made leaving nothing short of torture. We had Mark and Billy waiting in the solarium mainly to spare Mark the emotions we were feeling. When we came out I was doing my best not to let Billy see any tears, Margie was openly crying and I had my arm around her shoulder. Billy asked if we were okay and we told him we were, that we had done this many times before and while it never gets easy, it somehow remains doable. Once on the road home we kept busy talking about both Mark and Joey, which we found to be the best way to push the unhappiness of the situation aside and think of better thoughts.

Once we got home it was already time to prepare for our return trip to Baltimore the following day, this time anticipating our trip was different. Margie and I knew there was no work for us on Monday, we would be there to provide Joey with parental love and support. We spent the evening with Mark to make sure he knew we were there for him too, but I always suspected it was not enough. Margie and I knew there was still no way to effectively split ourselves in equal halves to provide the same amount of attention to both children. Life never promised to be fair and in this case the trade offs we were forced to make were to us -well beyond unfair. Mark Jr was still the little trooper, with maturity well beyond his years and he too worried about his little brother.

Joey over came his pneumonia quickly and he returned to the S.I.B.

unit at the Kennedy Institute and resumed his therapy. During his first day back he was again tested to see what he could safely eat or drink by mouth. Until the test was done he got his total nutritional requirements through that damn tube. We were pleased to see that Dr. Peggy Monahan would be the person doing the test and making the recommendations to best preserve our son's safety.

I was beginning to understand in a limited way how Joey's disease caused him to be his own worst enemy. Joey rarely got a pneumonia from some infectious process, more often then not it was because he aspirated something that did not cause him the coughing and gaging that it would cause everyone else. Margie and I both began to wonder how this was going to impact Joey's overall life expectancy. I personally knew from my training, that most healthy adults could not survive the number of Aspiration Pneumonia's he had already beaten. I could only imagine what Joey's lungs looked like with all the scaring left behind by each and every pneumonia.

Once again the days and weeks began to go by quickly and we hoped our boy would be coming home just as quickly. We could never forget how much of Joey's young life had been spent in hospitals and now it would add up to almost half of his four years. As Memorial Day approached we received a letter from The Women's World Weekly publication about their interest in Joey's story and asked us to call them. Margie and I both thought that with the international circulation of this paper we might just find a doctor that had dealt with this disease before and figured at this point it couldn't hurt to try. Margie called and made arrangements to meet with a reporter and photographer the following week while we were there for our training.

We met with the two people from Women's World, we answered their questions and allowed them to take pictures of Joey and Margie. We were told to expect this issue to hit the news stands in about a month. Now we were looking through that paper every time we waited in a grocery store check out line. When the story was finally published we bought the paper and we were extremely disappointed by what we read. The Women's World Weekly story made Joey sound like a monster, we couldn't believe what they wrote. The lady we met seemed like an honest and caring person, but we found she was nothing more then a tabloid reporter who distorted the facts and twisted the truth to sell more papers.

A few weeks later Margie got a call from her sister Sharon who lives in South Carolina, she asked why we didn't tell her The National Enquire was doing a story too. It turns out that The National Enquire picked up the story from the Associated Press wire and after they edited the story their way it was a much better piece that didn't make our son sound like the monster that Women's World Weekly portrayed him to be. The lessons we were being forced to learn from this experience were evolving in ways we never even considered.

Margie and I were learning that we couldn't trust people at face value the way we always did and that our naivete could haunt us for a very long time. We were finding that despite our eagerness to find that ever elusive answer for a disease from nowhere that doesn't even have a name. Now we had to be careful about who we could allow to help us answer our biggest question about Joey. Our ignorance about the intent of some people based on our own integrity was obviously off because we never imagined that someone could trash a child the way the Women's World Weekly did.

When Memorial Day weekend arrived we took Mark to visit Joey and we were surprised to find that a Telethon to help the children was being held at Johns Hopkins Medical Center. Margie and I were asked if it was okay to include Joey and to sign a release and the sad part was that we actually had to think about it before answering. We decided that this media outlet would most likely preserve Joey's dignity so we gave our approval This time the tables were slightly turned, we were not asking for help, the fact is that Joey was being asked too help. We knew that Joey had a heart of gold and he would like to be able to help in any way he could. We had a good time watching our boys play together and we savored these moments of love that even brothers have for each other. After spending a long day with Joey we headed home and spent the rest of the weekend missing a very important piece of our family, Joey.

The warm summer weather was again coming quickly and we again dreaded the weather we used to love so much. Then it happened, the day we had dreamt about was finally here and Joey was ready to come home. During one of our pervious trips Margie and I attended a discharge meeting to prepare for this day. We were told that the discharge would take longer then before, 4 days instead of 3 because we had more to learn. The Gastroenterologist (a doctor who treats stomach and intestinal problems) who was taking care of Joey's recently placed Gastrostomy Tube ordered a pump by which Joey would be feed. We had experience with the tube before, but even this had changed.

Joey was being fitted with a low profile Gastrostomy Button, which was much better then what we had experienced before. Instead of an 12 to 14 inch tube hanging out of Joey's belly that required a metal clamp to keep his stomach contents from leaking out, he now would have a button equipped with a cap and a valve to prevent the leakage from his stomach. This came with a catch, we would have to find a doctor to order and replace this device, which we didn't understand because we were taught how to replace the old tube and this device was even easier to change. We also had to find a medical supply company in our area that could provide the Kangaroo Pump that would feed Joey over longer periods of time and regulate the rate of formula he would receive by the hour. We also had to unsure that we were up to speed with regard to the behavior modification techniques we had learned over the last six months.

The day to begin getting Joey discharged was finally here and while this admission had taken almost six months to complete it again, felt more like a lifetime. Margie and I spent four days going over what we had learned both medically and behaviorally to hopefully prevent any future admissions in Baltimore. We were both pleased once again with all the improvements we saw in Joey. His behavior was well under control he was using sign language better then ever and more appropriately. The only thing that was not accomplished was the toilet training and for this Lynn was very apologetic, because she really believed she would be able to train him Margie and I both told her that we thought it had something to do with his neurologic deficit and he probably did not get the same sensations to indicate a need to use the bathroom.

When we were ready to leave, saying goodbye was a bitter-sweet for us because we regarded Lynn, Annie and the other nurses and aids as friends. These were people that we laughed and cried with, that cared for our youngest son for the last six months and did so in a way that any parent would approve of. We had an appreciation for these people that was special as well as a profound admiration for the work they do so well and successfully. When we finally left we knew that we would miss these people that were so helpful we also knew that Joey would miss them too.

I know it must sound crazy but to us the staff at The Kennedy Institute's Self Injurious Behavior Unit were like family and to Joey they were mom and dad most of the time, for the past six months. Although we knew it was not goodbye because we would be in touch frequently and Lynn would come to our home to check on Joey, we all hugged and with a bitter sweet feeling we left. The craziest part was the fact that we couldn't wait for this day to come and now that it was here our emotions were so mixed.

When we left for home I'm not sure what Joey was thinking, but I could imagine that he wasn't really sure what was happening and I actually wondered if he even remembered home. Once we got home Joey seemed somewhat lost by the way he carefully explored what must have been to him a new environment. With Joey finally home it was time to pick up where we had left off almost six long months ago. I was able to start working full time at the Summit Surgical Center and my wife and I were looking forward to my bringing home bigger pay checks.

By now we had a very disruptive chapter of our lives behind us and from our past experience we knew better then ask "what's next"? I don't think we even wanted to know the answer to that question, but we already knew there would be problems to face in the future regardless of our best efforts and intentions. Margie and I came to expect problems with Joey from all the repeated hospitalizations for various reasons. We already faced the possibility of losing our youngest son too many times in the past, for us this was becoming a normal part of our lives that we somehow learned to cope with.

Margie and I also began to take stock of our relationship and we both knew our marriage was not what it should have been We were wrapped up in a life style that was riddled with problems and this was causing us to lose touch with each other. I was still seeing a counselor every two weeks so I asked for advice and what I got probably saved our marriage. I quickly realized that it was all commonsense and my wife and I started to make some very minor changes to keep our relationship healthy. I first have to say that without the willingness to work together to improve what was never in real danger, we would have reached the dangerous point that can cause a good marriage to fail.

My wife and I came to the conclusion that despite what we had always been taught, that a house is the biggest investment we will ever make, is simply untrue. At least for us, our marriage was and still is the biggest investment we will ever make, which as you know is not a monetary investment, but rather an investment of time and effort. We figured that if we ever bought a house, we would do all the work and maintenance necessary to keep it in good shape, mainly because we didn't want to live in a dump and to protect our investment. We discovered marriage is in many ways the same and if we weren't willing to do the necessary work to maintain our relationship then we could not expect it to continue to work.

Margie and I started to make small changes in the way we did things. The first thing we did was to start having what we call a date night. We would chose one night a week when we would get a sitter for the boys and go out, sometimes it might just be a walk around the mall and other times it would be for a nice dinner out. The most important thing for us was to get out together to allow us to remember why we fell in love and got married in the first place. We found that by doing this we helped our marriage to grow stronger and all we were really doing was maintaining the foundation on which our relationship was built.

I won't lie and tell you we never fought because we had fights just like every other couple, at times we had some blood thirsty fights to the point that separation was considered, but somehow we never let it go that far. We also started to follow some guide line with respect to our arguments, I consider these rules to be the Geneva Convention of marital disagreements. To follow these we both had to mature a little, because during a fight it can be easy to forget for the moment that your opponent is someone you hopefully love and respect deeply. We stopped the childish name calling and personal attack strategies, but the toughest rules to follow by far are still; it's okay to agree to disagree (nobodies perfect) and assigning blame doesn't do much more then relieve your personal guilt. I freely admit that it's not always easy, but nothing of value ever comes easy, maybe that's why I call it work?

For our family, our lives were anything but average or normal so creativity was a very necessary addition to the glue that bound our family together. We had to make a choice; we can survive these ordeals as a family, or we could try to do it individually and alone. The choice might seem clear, but with the things we had already seen it's much too easy to get wrapped up in your own little pity party and forget who else is in it with you. It's really not fair to think your personal brand of hell is worse then anyone else's, the fact is, hell is hell. The only real difference is what you call hell and where it comes from.

After three years sense the onset of Joey's disease, we had barely scratched the surface of the education we would get, for us the lessons came here and there, without ever realizing that you were learning something. The weird part is that earning a degree from The University of Hard

Knocks doesn't require any studying, in fact you don't even enroll, this school somehow finds you and just starts teaching you. I can honestly say that this school provides the best real life education available anywhere in the world.

Our challenges with Joey would begin to change in ways we never could have imagined and our lives would have to change in ways we never could have anticipated to accommodate our youngest son's life.

Chapter 6

Our family was finally together at home where we belonged and Joey's admission in Baltimore was behind us. It was the hottest part of the summer and Margie and I worried about how the heat might effect Joey. Even with the cooling vest we were still apprehensive about taking Joey outside in the sun, so we made some minor changes with respect to what we carried with us anytime we went anywhere. We started to carry cold water to spray on Joey's skin and hair, an umbrella for shade and our trusty thermometer. These items were always on hand because of Joey's experience of summers past, we were not taking any chances. On the bright side we took some trips to the Jersey shore and even spent some time on the beach, but best of all was the time we spent on the boardwalk.

Mark and Joey both loved the rides on the amusement piers and Margie and I loved taking them on the rides. There was more junk food, burgers and fudge then anyone should ever eat, along with games to win things (mostly stuffed animals). The only real change we made going to the shore were the extra items we carried and the time of day we would leave. We would wait till afternoon to leave so the time we could spend in the sun was limited, but we still had enough time to have a great time. I was working four ten hour days and enjoyed having three days off every week and earning full time paychecks. Mark Jr was about to start 2nd grade and Joey was going to start a preschool program that was ran by the Sea Shore House of Philadelphia for disabled children. Margie was being a nervous mother that seemed to require her to worry about every little thing, especially Joey. At the same time we were both happy about Joey starting school and we liked the idea that he would get more therapy, more frequently then he could get at home. I was beginning to feel like we might get our slice of the American dream after all.

The remainder of the year went well with only one or two short hospitalizations for bad colds. The holidays came and went with us savoring the fact that we were all home to enjoy them together. Christmas was always great but now I was beginning to dread the New Year because I knew that it just had to come with bigger and better challenges.

The New year came and brought 1991 and we could only hope that it might somehow be better then the last few years and it looked like it would. The first few months went well and by early spring Margie's attorney called to make arrangements for the depositions about her accident, he also told us he expected to settle the case by mid summer.

As planned we attended one deposition and got a settlement offer shortly after, our attorney negotiated a better offer and we settled, but not without a hitch. Our own insurance company would not pay any of the medical bills associated with her short term memory loss, due to brain trauma. They were blaming stress produced by caring for Joey and not her head injury, so we had to arbitrate this discrepancy to get the last 25% of the total settlement that had been put in escrow for the remaining bills.

When Margie finally got her settlement we decided it was time to buy a house and now we had some money for a down payment. We began shopping around fora house with a small yard we could afford, hopefully in a quite neighborhood with decent schools. We found a house that we liked in September that year and we planned on closing the deal in mid November, pending professional inspection and mortgage approval. The latter was our biggest concern because of our recent bankruptcy, but reaffirming our debts and only having medical bills discharged helped and we were able to secure a mortgage.

The arbitration with our insurance company was held in October and was to say the least a disgrace for our own insurance to make the argument they made. After the 2 attorneys finished asking Margie and I questions, I asked the arbitrator if l could ask the attorney that represented the insurance carrier a question? The arbitrator allowed me to ask my question provided I was not disrespectful. I asked this attorney why we were not being turned into the prosecutors office and charged with attempted insurance fraud? I followed by saying that as an officer of the court she had a responsibility to file this charge if what she was saying was true. I never did get an answer but I did get a knowing smile from both our attorney and the arbitrator.

The following day Margie got a call from her attorney telling her that a decision had been made and we would get 100% of the money in escrow. Margie told me she wanted to get away without the children and made arrangements to get some respite care (24 hour nursing care) for Joey. We went to a couples only resort in the Pocono mountains of Pennsylvania called Cove Haven. This place was something special, it was an all inclusive resort that would serve you breakfast in your room or the dinning room or both and all you can eat sit down dinners. There were plenty of activities available, Miniature Golf, Boccie Ball, Tennis, Rachet Ball, Archery, Billiards, Ice Skating and a Swimming Pool with Hot Tubes and a bar, all indoors.

There were also games ran by a social director that were fun to either watch or take part in. Every night they had great shows in the nightclub and more games with the social director. The guest rooms were absolutely gorgeous and plush, in the room we had a working fireplace, a heart shaped Jacuzzi for two, a Sauna and our own private swimming pool. These rooms were pure luxury and the staff catered to our every want or need. Margie and I had a wonderful time and didn't want to leave this beautiful mountain setting.

In November 1991 we made settlement on the house we were buying and we paid rent through December to give us time to do some work in the house, we painted some walls, shampooed the carpets and I put a one piece linoleum floor in Joey's new bedroom (to make cleaning up formula spills easy). I was now sure that we were finally living the American Dream and thought the toughest chapters of our lives were behind us. We decided to start moving after the Thanksgiving holiday so I made arrangements at work for an extra day off to make the move.

Thanksgiving was even more special then ever before, we had our family together, Joey was doing surprisingly well and we were ready to move into a house of our own. This year we had been given so much to be thankful for and that helped us appreciate the true meaning of the holiday even more then ever before. After the holiday we started packing and moving, Margie and I were shocked by the amount of stuff we had accumulated during the 8 years we lived in our apartment.

After we finished moving and getting our new home fixed up and decorated the way we wanted we felt like we had been given a tiny slice of heaven on earth. When we were finally settled in, we started preparing for Christmas and this year we had a house and yard to decorate instead of an apartment with one window and a balcony worth decorating. We also made sure to give our boys the best Christmas ever with lots of toys and games, this year was truly special and we made sure the boys understood why. We always tried our best to convey the true meaning of the season to our children, trying to help them understand that it was more about the birth of Jesus and the gifts and toys were just a bonus.

When Christmas arrived we celebrated like never before, while savoring every second of the holiday that we could, it was truly a wonderful day that we wished could last forever. Our children spent their day playing with as many toys as they possibly could and I spent a large part of the day assembling toys and preparing dinner (I am the designated cook for holiday dinners). We had a big family dinner with friends and family that helped make the day even more special. Like all good things this too came to an end, I had to work the next day so reality set in and I prepared myself for work in my usual way.

The following day at work was uneventful and slow because of a very light surgical schedule, we actually finished early and even left about an hour early. As I drove home that day I was looking forward to playing with the boys and their new toys and gifts they had received the day before. I didn't have a clue that our world was about to be turned upside down and twisted iri. ways that I'm sure would have made Satan proud.

I arrived home about an hour early and sat on the sofa with Joey while Margie finished making dinner. Afterwards I again sat with Joey on the sofa, but now I noticed that his fingernails were a light shade of blue, so I asked Margie to take him to the hospital, while I got a shower and found someone to watch Mark so I could get to the hospital with my wife and son. I called my mother to ask her to come over and watch Mark and told her why, while I was waiting for her I showered and changed and for some unknown reason I took my boss's home phone number and put it in my pocket. I was ready to leave before my mother arrived and the phone rang, it was Margie crying, telling me to get to the hospital as soon as I could that Joey's problem was critical. As I hung up my mother came in and started asking questions, I told her I would call her later, that it was evidently real bad.

When I got to the hospital I went straight to Joey and found him Intubated (a tube down the throat to allow mechanical respiration) on a Ventilator (a machine that breathes for you), because of this Joey was heavily sedated to help keep him calm so the doctors could do what was necessary. Margie was beside herself with fear and I knew Joey was in more danger then ever before. A nurse took my wife and I to a small room to try to explain what was going on. Joey had a very severe pneumonia and the C02 (carbon dioxide) in his blood was critically high over 80% (the normal range is between 35% and 45%) while the oxygen level in his blood was dangerously low only about 75 to 80% (the normal is 90% to 99%) and this is why he needed to be put on a Ventilator for artificial respiration. The nurse told us that their team of critical care doctors were working to get him stabilized so he could be transferred to St. Christopher's Hospital for Children in Philadelphia.

After hearing all this Margie and I were just plain scared for our son's life and we just could not believe it had to happen the day after the best Christmas we ever had. I called my boss Bissy and told her what was happening and that I would not be at work the following day, she told me not to worry about work and to call if she could help. Our world was spinning completely out of control and we had no idea what to do other then pray and even praying was incredibly hard to do, it was all but impossible to even think clearly.

While all this was going on the doctors were trying to decide if Joey should be taken by Ambulance or flown by Helicopter to St. Christopher's. After some debate it was decided that while he could get to Philly in about ten minutes by Helicopter, there was very little room to work inside the chopper. They figured that it would be safer to make the move by Ambulance because of the extra room in case thing started going bad on the way. After only about 45 minutes the St. Christopher's Transport Teem arrived and as usual it included a doctor and nurse along with two Emergency Medical Technicians (EMT' s) one of which was driving. Joey was quickly prepared for the trip and I was told what roads would be used to stay as close as they could to the various hospitals on the way.

The EMT that was driving explained that if a problem arose during the trip they would use the facilities at which ever hospital was closest, Joey was put in the ambulance and mom was allowed to stay with him for the ride while I followed. I was told not to try to keep up with them because they would be moving fast and I should drive safely. I'm not sure but I think a hunk of wood, would have listened better. There was no way I was going to let that ambulance out of my sight, at least not while it was carrying my son who might well be dying and St. Christopher's had moved to a new building that I had no idea how to find.

We all arrived safely at the same time, while I parked our car Joey was rushed to the Critical Care Unit (CCU). When I found the CCU and Joey I was amazed by the flurry of activity around him and I must admit it was all quite scarey, all the while we feared for his life. Margie and I were like a pair of frightened like a Deer caught in the headlights of an oncoming car, we just did not know what to do. The reality was, there was nothing we could do but pray and our confusion was unlike anything we had ever experienced before.

After Joey was settled in a doctor came and talked to us, he explained that Joey's condition was very critical and his only chance of survival would be through the use of the Ventilator (Vent). The doctor told us Joey would be kept sedated and comfortable until he could be taken off the Vent and breathing adequately enough on his own. Margie and I only had one question we wanted an answer for; will he survive? To this the doctor answered honestly, I don't know, it's to soon too tell. I called my mother and told her we would not be home that night and did my best to explain what was going on. Naturally she had more questions then I could even begin to answer and told her I would pass on the answers as soon as they were known. At the moment I'm not sure I knew my own name, the only thing I fully understood was fear and our total lack of control. By the time the light of the next day came we still knew nothing and we were becoming exhausted, we just wanted to be there incase Joey woke up so he would know his mother and father was there for him. I called home and told my mother we should be home sometime after dinner and we stayed by Joey's bed all day. Sometime around 7 or 8 o'clock that evening we finally got home, we had both been awake for more then 36 hours and needed to get some sleep, but as tired as we were we didn't sleep well because of our worries about our son. Now Mark was at his grandmother's house and I called George to tell him what had happened and to ask for his assistance with Mark. He said he could be there by early afternoon and he would pick Mark up to bring him home so he could play with his friends and his new toys.

When we got back to the hospital we found Joey awake which was initially a welcome sight, but after a few minutes we realized the problem had grown and had become.even more dangerous then ever. Margie and I found him staring out the window looking very sad and after we each gave him a hug and kiss he still stared out the window, he would not acknowledge our presence at all. Joey didn't want anything to do with anything and we thought our absolute worst fear was realized, Joey had given up and he seemed like he was just waiting to die. I don't care what anyone ever says, this is without a doubt the worst thing a parent could ever witness. Margie and I both got in bed on each side of him trying to give him the love and support that might give him some hope, but he just wanted to be left alone.

Our hearts were shattered and sinking quickly, but Margie and I with all our fear unlike anything we ever felt before, were not going to let him give up without a fight. We didn't know how, but we were determined to put the will to live back in his heart. We spent the day with him, trying to get him to play, but we got nowhere, he just stared out that window as if looking for the Angel to come and take him home to God. His mother and I knew if we couldn't change his mind and get him to start fighting he would certainly die.

We stayed with him till late at night praying and hoping we would see at least a glimmer of hope, but the hope never came that day. Joey was fast asleep and the doctors thought he was making good progress physically, but these guys weren't even looking at his emotional state. Margie and I decided that we would go home and gather up some of his brand new toys that he never got a chance to play with after Christmas. We picked the toys that we hoped he would not be able to ignore and took them to the hospital with us early the next morning.

We got to the hospital by 6 in the morning because we didn't want Joey to be awake too long before we arrived. When we got to his bed his was just waking up, mom and I each gave him a big hug and kiss, but we still got the same response, he was looking for that Angel that we prayed would wait just a little longer. The morning routine in the CCU was quite busy and we were asked to get some breakfast or take a walk to allow the doctors and nurses to do all the things that they needed to do. They told us to try to give them about an hour to get him ready for the day and they did have a lot to do. We got breakfast and indigestion at the same time, then went to the chapel to pray in an effort to restore our hope and give them the hour they requested. We got back in a little under an hour and stood out of the way in front of the window he was staring through.

The morning activity was finally finished and we took the toys and tried to get Joey interested in playing. Margie and I took turns playing with different toys and after about an hour he finally gave in. We caught his interest with a learning toy that helps children learn to read, a battery powered gadget that says a word associated with a picture. Joey finally started playing and before too long his eyes lit-up as he started to have fun with this toy, better still he was now looking for us to play with him. At that moment we began to have hope that he might start fighting to live.

I can't even begin to express the feelings we had, it was the craziest mix anyone could ever imagine. Our youngest son is in a bed with tubes in his arms, another down his throat that was hooked to a machine that breathed for him and wires everywhere to monitor his heart, lungs and blood gases. At the same time we felt a kind of joy that I don't think winning a multi-million dollar lottery could bring. I know this must sound sick, but try to understand that we just watched our son go from wanting to die to having hope of living. They say men never experience tears of joy, I here to tell you different. I cried those tears along with my wife as we hugged our boy with all the love we could muster. Our plan worked and somehow we knew Joey would survive. We again stayed until he was asleep that night before returning home to our oldest son and to get some rest. George was now at the house helping out with Mark and keeping him busy having fine and providing the distraction we hoped he would. Everyday everyone asked questions that we didn't have answers for, we could only tell them that the best we could do was to pray for him. We didn' t know what to tell Mark, he was only nine years old and we knew his understanding of this would be limited at best. Beside that, his only real question was; is Joey going to be okay? We told him he would, but the reality was that we hoped he would, all the while we weren't sure how else to protect Mark from the grim reality we faced.

The next day at the hospital we got a treat, Joey was no longer hooked to that Ventilator, he was breathing on his own. Joey's nurse told us that while the nurses were all giving their report during the shift change through the night, they thought they herd him cry out. The nurse said that they couldn't understand this, because the Endotracheal tube that was down his throat and allowed the Ventilator to get air into his lungs, also prevents a person from making sounds with their voice. So needless to say he was checked out quickly and found to be holding the tube in his hand. Joey somehow found a way to free his hand from the restraint they were using to prevent him from pulling the tube, all while being under the influence of Intravenous Valium.

Margie and I looked at each other with ear to ear smiles, to us this meant he was fighting to live and this was the best feeling of all. Joey's pneumonia was beginning to clear and we started to think he was out of the woods. I called Bissy at work and gave her the news and told her I would be at work the following day, everything just felt right, but feelings can be deceiving and this time they were. We stayed with Joey until night before going home and I was looking forward to getting back to work. The next day I went to work and started my day as usual, I got changed into my scrubs and got my room assignment and surgical schedule for the day. Our first case was starting a half hour later then normal 7:30am instead of 7am, so I got a cup of coffee and went into the locker room to call home, to see what Margie had heard from the hospital when she called that morning. Margie told me that Joey's Co2 blood level started to rise over night and he had to be intubated again and put back on the Ventilator again. Needless to say this was not the news I had hoped for, in fact it was quite devastating, but I was at work and I wanted to stay through the day.

I went to my assigned operating room and began opening up the instruments for our first case. While I was doing this the circulating nurse, Susan and anesthesiologist, Donna came in and immediately asked about Joey. I tried with all my might to just tell them what was going on, hoping I could go on with my work. I told them about the last couple of days and when I got to the part about him going back on the Vent, I lost it. Trying not to cry in front of my coworkers I excused myself and headed for the locker room. I don't know why I did this because I knew that Susan and Donna would both be on my heels and they were, only because they cared. They both walked into the men's locker room to find me, not caring if a doctor was getting dressed.

They took me by the hand and led me into Donna 's office and did their best to console me, I felt like a fool sobbing like a baby and not being able to control my emotions. Bissy also came in and after I calmed down a little bit, Bissy took me into her office to talk with me, she told me that under the circumstances I needed to be with my wife and son. She also told me all the reason's and cliches' about why it's okay for me to be crying. Then she said, if I wasn't' t able to drive, that she would drive me home. I assured her I could drive and gave her a hug and thanked her, before I left I went back to my assigned operating room to thank both Susan and Donna. As I made my way back to the locker room I was stopped by a few other nurses I worked with and given hugs and told that Joey and my family would be in their prayers and they wished me well.

When I returned home it was still early morning, so after explaining to Margie what had happened we went to the hospital. After some time, one of the many doctors involved in Joey's care came in to check on him. When he finished examining our son Margie and I began asking questions, only this time the doctor had no real explanation for us. The doctor was genuinely perplexed but he told us what he did know, which wasn't much. He told us that Joey's pneumonia was clearing up nicely, but they expected his need for the Ventilator to diminish as well and could not explain why he was unable to breath adequately enough on his own. We were told that the hope was that as Joey got stronger his need for artificial respiration would then disappear.

During the day, the way the Ventilator worked was changed, it provided positive air pressure for his lungs, basically it was continuously blowing a small amount of air into his lungs to help keep them from collapsing again. This also meant that Joey was doing most of the work himself to breath and the machine was only offering support. At night however, as Joey slept, he needed the machine to take over and do the breathing for him. This was the problem that the doctors were having such a hard time understanding, for my wife and I this was as confusing as anything we ever tried to understand and could not, to me it was almost like trying to understand Quantum Physics with out the benefit of a teacher.

Day after day nothing changed and the doctors had very little to offer in the way of an explanation and for over a week the doctors didn't even know what they were seeing, or what to test for. I was grasping for straws and called Susan Hyman in Baltimore and tried to explain what was happening. Dr. Hyman being the caring doctor she is called the hospital and talked to the attending physician to get as much clinical data as she could. Susan then talked to the experts at Johns Hopkins University in hopes of finding some helpful information. Unfortunately nobody had much in the way of suggestions to hunt for an answer that was as elusive as the disease that continued to try to take our youngest son away from us.

Then after two weeks of nothing more then supportive care and common sense medicine (which is not very common for doctors who have very little in the way of common sense), one of the Neurologists came up with the idea of doing a Co2 challenge test. To do this Joey would have the tube taken out of his throat and made to breath a high level of Co2 to see of his breath rate increased. The doctor explained that this test would simulate vigorous physical activity. Almost like running, were the muscles burn lots of Oxygen and create high levels of Carbon

Dioxide, causing a person to breath harder to blow off the high levels of Co2 to be replaced by the Oxygen in the air we breath. The test would be scheduled for that afternoon at his bedside and as the time got near there was some very unusual equipment brought in, along with doctors, nurses and technicians from various ~· specialties. There was a Pulmonologist, Neurologist, Cardiologist, an EEG Technician, Respiratory Therapists and a host of nurses. Needless to say there was not much room for Margie and I but we managed to stay out of the way and watch this unusual test. When everything was in place and ready to go Joey was extubated (the breathing tube was removed) and then came the one of scariest things we ever witnessed. Our son was gasping for air, the look of fear on his face was of pure terror, he was wheezing loudly and struggling for every breath. The doctors, nurses and technicians worked calmly and quickly to administer a medication that he could inhale to help him breath easier. This stuff was like magic and started to work almost instantly, Joey began to calm down and breath normally, unfortunately these are the experiences a parent never forgets and your brain seems to be branded with the memory forever.

After this flurry of activity calmed and a more normal pace started, a nurse explained what we had just witnessed. It turns out that the tube that had been down Joey's throat for two weeks had caused a great deal of inflamation and swelling causing his airway to close considerably and there was even a name for this condition, they called it a Stridor. I asked what the miracle drug was that worked so well and was told it was just plain old Cortisone.

The Co2 challenge started and we watched as they did the test, not understanding anything we saw. Joey was made to breath the Co2 thru a mask, much like an Oxygen mask and he was monitored for breath rate, heart rate while also running an EEG to monitor his brain waves. One of the hopes was that Joey would be a candidate for a device called a Diaphragmatic Pace Maker, that instead of stimulating his heart to beat normally, would instead stimulate his Diaphragm to help him breath normally and help him regulate the level of Co2 in his blood. Unfortunately the test ruled that possibility out and the results were known immediately at the conclusion of the test.

The Neurologist and Pulmonologist talked briefly and then took Margie and I to a nearby conference room. Once there we were told what the results were and given some options. There were only two options and each were not good, in fact they were at least horrifying if nothing else.

They explained that we could do nothing and Joey would surely die and they actually called that an option, or he could get a Tracheostomy (a hole in the base of his neck into his Trachea or windpipe) thru which a silicon device called a Trach (a curved tube only a few inches in length) would be inserted. The Trach would enable us to hook him up to a Ventilator, which at the time would only be needed while he slept, or while fighting a bad cold or pneunxmia During the day however he would need a humidifier to replace the moisture that is provided by his upper airway (nose and sinuses). We were also told that they would like us to have an answer in only 48 hours.

Naturally Margie and I had some questions and the most important of which was; how would this affect Joey's overall quality oflife? Would he be bed ridden, or could he still be a 6 year old and play like the child he is? The answers were not what we expected and we were told he could do everything any other child could do except play in a sand box or go swimming. This was good, but the decision was still one of the toughest we would ever face. To us we were being asked to play God and make a choice that would have such a profound effect Joey, everyday for the rest of his life. We also wanted to know if we decided to insert the Trach; how long would he live? The doctor's best guess was probably not much more then two years. We were told that the problem was in his brain, that he somehow lost his ability to regulate the CO_2 in his blood while he slept, that the condition was very rare and the exact cause was still unknown. They only had past experience to draw answers from and the two years were based on other children who had similar conditions in the past.

Talk about a world spinning out of control, Margie and I were faced with making a choice we felt was best left to God and they wanted or answer quickly, at least to us, 48 hours was just not enough time. We talked and questioned each other and neither of us knew what to do or say, we both wished Joey could understand this and tell us what he wanted, but he could not. We weren't even sure how to tell Mark Jr of this choice, but we also knew that he should not be left totally out of the decision. We were lost, plain and simple and could not even find a way to help us make the choice. We could do nothing and let him die, or we could keep him alive for a couple of years, with the aid of machines and these were his only options.

After some talking and brainstorming between my wife and I we decided to get the opinion of a child, after all we were adults and could not even begin to imagine how child would think. When we got home that night, we sat down with Mark and his big buddy George and tried to explain the situation as delicately as we could. We told him what each choice meant and simply asked him; if this was you what would you want us to do? Just asking a 9 year old this question didn't seem fair, but somehow it seemed necessary. Mark started crying, as were Margie and me, but he quickly asked the question that was most important to him. Could he still play and have fun? We told him he could and he quickly said, then I would want the operation. Mark understood this better then we could have hoped, he told his mother and I, if he couldn't play and have fun then he would rather die. Margie and I already knew what the choice would be and Mark's input confirmed what we were thinking. The following morning we signed the necessary papers and the surgery was scheduled for the next day. We noticed that the breathing tube had not been replaced and asked his nurse about this. We were told that through the night his CO_2 level was being monitored closely as he slept and when the level of CO_2 began to rise, they would wake him up and make him angry, this in turn would make him breath harder and blow off the CO_2 that was accumulating. This of course meant that he was not getting the good restful sleep he needed, but it was only for two nights and we were more worried about his overall future. We spent as much time as we could with Joey, playing and helping him pass the time.

The following day we got to the hospital as early as we could so we could spend as much time as possible with him, before the surgery that would have such a profound effect on the rest of his life. Margie and I wanted to explain to Joey what was about to happen but we didn't know how or if he would even understand. When the people arrived that would take him to the operating room we did our best to tell him that when he woke up, he would have a hole in his throat that he would breath through and assured him that he would be okay. Margie and I walked with him as the orderly and nurse pushed his bed to the outer area of the operating room. We could tell that Joey was scared and didn't want to go but there was nothing we could do but let him know that his parents would be here when he woke up and how much we loved him.

The procedure was really quite simple would not take very long to complete) knew this from my own experience in the operating room and seeing this surgery first hand. As expected, after only about a half hour the surgeon came out and told us the operation was done and Joey did fine, he also told us that he would be in recovery for about an hour. Now we were hoping that Joey would not hate us, or feel like he was being punished, because of what we had allowed these doctors to do to him. Margie and I knew all to well that Joey's life had just been changed dramatically and wondered how long it would take him to adapt to this unexpected change in his life. We also knew we would be required to learn how to care for our youngest son and his newly acquired needs, as well as how to use all this new equipment.

When Joey woke up he didn't seem to be bothered by the Trach at all and we weren't sure this was because he was still groggy or because it really didn't matter that much to him. Now that the surgery was done, we were able to work toward him healing from this recent insult to his already fragile body. Margie and I would also start learning what we needed to know about his care and how to manage emergencies. The best part was that the worst was behind us and we could start working to getting Joey home where he belonged. After a few short days when I was comfortable that Joey was now stable, I called and made arrangements to return to work.

During the first few days we expected Joey to be irritated by the Trach in his neck and we thought he would try to pull it out. Margie and I also expected to see some depression, but we did not. Joey was still the cantankerous 6 year old we always knew him to be and he was happy. We don't know why but this Trach never seemed to matter much to our son, other then making it easier to ensure his ability to breath. We thought it would at least take some time for him to adapt to this new device, fact is he just didn't care about it. Joey did however continue to care about the things that were important to him, his brother, his parents, toys and cartoons. I guess to a child these are the things that keeps their world going around.

I returned to work a couple days later and really enjoyed the change of atmosphere, here I didn't have to make any life changing decisions, I only followed the orders of the surgeon that made all the choices. The only decisions I needed to make were which instruments we would need to perform the various surgeries that would be done in the room I was assigned to. This was almost like a vacation from the harsh reality that my family and myself were being forced to live.

About a month later Joey was getting ready to leave St. Christopher's Hospital which required Margie and I to attend the first discharge meeting. During the meeting the first question asked of us was; had we figured out which nursing home we wanted Joey to go to? We answered this with another question; why can't we try to care for him at home? We were told there was really no reason why we would not be able to care for him at home, but they wanted Joey to get some private duty nursing at home, because he was now a 24 hour job, 7 days a week.

My wife and I also needed to make some changes at home, because Joey's bedroom on the second floor of our house was no longer practical for him and all his equipment. Fortunately we had a small room just off the kitchen that Margie was using for a music room, she wanted to be a country singer. We decided that we would use Joey's original bedroom for the music room and use the room off the kitchen for Joey's bedroom. We did it this way for a couple of reasons, first there was a lot of equipment that our boy would now need and we would also have medical supplies delivered weekly. My wife and I also wanted to keep some of our privacy and if we had a nurse with Joey just down the hall, our privacy would have been lost. I guess we were lucky to be able to make these minor changes in our home to accommodate Joey and his needs along with all the equipment he would come home with.

The hospital social worker made arrangements with a nursing agency to provide the nursing care and she also contacted a medical supply company to get and maintain the necessary equipment. This would take another two or three weeks to get together. Once the arrangements were made we had another discharge meeting, during which we met with the manager, Beth and one of the nurses, Marilyn from the nursing agency that would be doing the case. We also met with the Respiratory Therapist, Guy that worked for the medical supply company, that would be responsible to supply and maintain the equipment, to meet Joey's needs.

During the meeting it was decided that the Respiratory Therapist from the medical supply company would bring the Ventilator we would use at home for Joey, to the hospital and set it up. The hospital would use this equipment for Joey, for at least a week before he would be discharged, to ensure safety. The following day Guy brought the Ventilator to the hospital and set it up for Joey, this was one of the steps needed to get our son home. Margie and I had to spend a night in the hospital to ensure that we could meet his needs at home. We did his total care that night, everything from suctioning his lungs to hooking him up to the Ventilator, this was to show to doctors and nurses that we had learned how to care for him without the help of a doctor, nurse or technician.

The night we spent caring for our son went smoothly and the hardest part was just staying awake. The doctors were now confidant that we would be able to care for Joey and meet his special needs, so they went forward with the discharge. All this equipment and stuff we needed to learn how to use sounds pretty complicated, but it was really quite simple. Everything was now in place and Joey was only a few days from home.

Now that we had a discharge date Margie and I made arrangements for a welcome home party for Joey. We ordered lunch meat trays from our local delicatessen and a full sheet cake from our favorite bakery, along with a half keg of Root Beer. Margie had also called the anchor person Kathy from our local TV news station, who sent a news crew to cover the party and interview our family. When the day came for Joey to be discharged and come home I was working and I think my coworkers were almost as excited as I was. Margie and a friend picked Joey up at the hospital and brought him to the Summit Surgical Center were I worked, mainly to thank my co-workers for their prayers and support. Now Margie and I had a surprise waiting for us at my job, my coworkers had taken a collection to help us off set our lose of income and the expense of going to Philadelphia everyday. They also bought a cake to celebrate Joey's coming home, they collected and gave us almost $1,500.00 in a card that was signed by everyone I worked with and most of the surgeons that brought cases to the Summit. Margie and I couldn't even find the words to thank them enough for their kindness and genuine concern. They all new about the party we were throwing because they were all invited, but they told me that they wanted to do something special to help. I told them they already did everyday, it is called caring and support and they gave me plenty of that.

The welcome home party was held on the first Saturday Joey was home and I did most of the running to pick up the cake, food and Root Beer. As I went to each store I was again surprised, not a single one would let me pay for the stuff we ordered, they were all friends of ours and wanted to contribute to Joey's home coming celebration. As we were setting up for the party, George was feeding me shots of Root Beer Schnapps and not being a drinker, had me half drunk in no time. The Channel6 News crew showed up, the anchor was a young lady named Lucy. Margie and I were interviewed together and then Lucy took Mark Jr into Joey's new bedroom to interview him alone. Nether Margie or I knew what Mark was asked or what he said until we watched the news that night. When he was finished he was all smiles because he was going to be on the 11 o'clock news, which I'm sure thrilled him to the bone.

Before long the party was in full swing and everybody had a great time and we all agreed that this was a real reason to celebrate. The two year prognosis was lost to our happiness of having the chance to love both of our children a little longer, besides Margie and I were determined to prove the doctors wrong. We flat out refused to dwell on the uncertainty of Joey's future and learned to accept what each new day brought, one day at a time.

The party lasted several hours and went well into the night, everyone came to help us celebrate this magnificent event. We had our families and friends together and our neighbors from our relatively new neighborhood. To someone driving by that didn't know what was going on, they must have thought we were celebrating an event like the homeowner winning the Presidential election or the million dollar lottery. This party had a special meaning to my family that I'm sure was missed by most everyone in attendance. My family was celebrating Joey's still being alive and everyone else was celebrating his coming home. This was exactly the way we wanted it and best of all, everyone had a good reason to smile and be happy, especially Joey.

Chapter 7

It was the later part of the spring and the days were getting hot and humid again, only now things were different. Margie and I still made a point to get Joey out but now we had more equipment to carry, along with the cooling vest, thermometer, spray bottle with cold water we now had an Ambu bag (a manually operated bag to provide artificial respiration), a replacement Trach tube, portable suction machine, suction catheters, sterile saline ampules and a Pulse Oximeter (an electronic device to monitor Oxygen levels in the blood). Just going out to the local mall was becoming more of a chore, then simply going out. Margie and I already decided not to allow these new hurdles keep Joey down, after all we decided to use machines to keep our son alive and it was up to his mother and I to make sure he had a life worth living.

As summer approached our apprehension over Joey's safety grew as well, we knew all too well of his problems with the summer heat and his latest problems only compounded our fears. After some adjustment and careful planning to carry all the equipment with us, our ability to get Joey out continued. We now had something new to deal with, we had a nurse in our home every evening for twelve hours daily to monitor and care for our son so my wife and I could get some sleep. The nurses we had were all good at what they did and they took care of all of Joey's needs through the night, but now we had to learn how to cope with our loss of privacy. We learned quickly to use our date nights to talk about our private matters, we were just doing whatever we could to make the best of this situation. After making these adjustments life continued and became as normal as possible. I was working my four ten hour days and Margie was doing her best to maintain control at home.

The summer came and went quickly and smoothly, but as fall approached our son began to develop a new problem. Joey was having problems tolerating his feeds, at first he would lay on his side with his knees drawn up to his chest and retch with dry heaves. Naturally we took him to the doctor, who ordered some tests and wrote a prescription to calm his stomach, this however could only be given by injection. We filled the prescription and got a box of syringes with needles and the medicine. Now we had something to give him to help him be more comfortable and this stuff did help, but it also made him sleepy, which under the circumstances was okay with us.

We got the tests done but as usual didn't show anything and now the problem had progressed to vomiting. Joey's Nissen Fundoplication (the surgery done when to stop reflux of stomach contents) had slipped. Margie and I were taking our boy to different Gastroenterologists trying to fmd someone to help our son. On top of this Joey was beginning to aspirate his stomach contents again, he was also beginning to get aspiration pneumonia again.

After many hospitalizations and tests at three major medical centers St. Christopher's Hospital, Children's Hospital of Philadelphia and Cooper Medical Center we came up empty, with one small exception. Children's Hospital of Philadelphia did get a positive test for reflux, but the doctors told us that our son was such a high surgical risk that they were unwilling to correct the problem This had me quite confused, these were the guys that would separate conjoined twins with less then a 1% chance of survival, but Joey would be left to die because of the risk associated with the surgery. Margie and I knew there had to be an option so we called Susan in Baltimore and explained the problem. After hearing all the details she promised to see what she could find and call us back. By now Thanksgiving had come and gone and we really didn't feel very thankful at the time. Christmas also flew by with us more worried about Joey being sick and getting very frequent pneumonia's, then being able to enjoy the holiday season.

Shortly after the New Year we got a call from Dr. Axlerod in New York, she explained that she had gotten a call from Susan about Joey's problem Dr. Axlerod explained that there was a Dr. Ginsberg at N.Y.U. that could do the surgery to correct Joey's problem, with regard to Joey vomiting and aspirating stomach contents. She made it clear that this would protect his lungs by stopping the aspiration pneumonia's that our son was suffering all too often. With our permission Dr. Axlerod would talk to Dr. Ginsberg and possibly schedule a date for surgery and she would call back in a day or two. Dr. Axlerod called back as promised and gave us the details we were hoping for, she gave us an admission date and a surgical date, along with information about hotels near the hospital that offered discounts for the families of patients. Joey was to be admitted on Monday March 1st and have the surgery on Wednesday March 3rct and barring complications would come home a week later on Wednesday March 10 th.

Margie and I had little more then six weeks to make our plans for the trip and arrange for someone to watch Mark Jr for a week. I called George who agreed to keep Mark at his place down the shore for as long as we needed. Margie found us a room across the street for the hospital for a very reasonable price for the ten days we planned for Joey's stay in New York. The biggest problem we now faced for the trip was Parking for the car, the hotel we were staying in did not offer Parking and private lots in New York City were incredibly expensive. After some thought we decided to take the train from Philadelphia and use public transportation in New York if it was necessary. We were able to make our plans quickly and without problems. Margie submitted the required paperwork to medicaid for approval of out of state treatment. Surprisingly the Medicaid approval was granted quickly and without question.

I remember asking Dr. Axlerod about the medicaid problems from the not to distant past and how Joey almost missed getting treatment at Johns Hopkins a year before. Dr. Axlerod told me not to worry about it because there are ways around their bureaucracy. The doctor told me that direct admission from another hospital could not be refused and if necessary we would take Joey to our local community hospital and get ambulance transport to N.Y.U. Medical Center in Manhattan. I guess Murphy's Law also works in reverse, if it can't be stopped, no one will try (medicaid included).

Now as the day to go to New York approaches we find ourselves not wanting to go, we wanted Joey's life protected, but we did not want our son to be forced to endure such a major surgery, we were also worried about his survival. Through the years we have learned that it never becomes easy even if it is your child's only chance at life, maybe because whatever surgery is being done always carries the risk of death.

February 26th, 1993 it was Friday and the last day I would work before taking a week off to be with our son for his week or so in N.Y.U.

Medical Center. Near the end of the day when our surgical schedule was finished and we were preparing for Monday and restocking our Surgical Suite, we felt what I can only describe as a heavy thud that briefly shook the building. Our maintenance man Rob and I went all over the building trying to find the cause of this, after an hour of searching everywhere and finding nothing before someone told us the news said, that we had a very minor Earthquake. In New Jersey Earthquakes are things that we only read about and rarely ever fee~ but this one we felt, fortunately we still didn't feel much. After I got home I watched our evening TV news and learned that the World Trade Center had been bombed. This was our first terrorist attack with a Truck Bomb parked under the building when it exploded, which closed a major Train Station in New York City. This news made us wonder if we would have to find a different mode of transportation to N.Y.U. On Saturday Joey got sick and started with the vomiting and retching, so we gave him a shot and hoped for the best. We called Dr. Axlerod to tell her about Joey being sick, she told us that if he was still sick tomorrow to call her and she would get Joey admitted a day earlier, Sunday instead of Monday. I called Amtrak to make sure the train was still going to Penn Station, it was, so our planned transportation was still a viable option. Early Sunday morning we woke up to find Joey just as sick as the day before, his nurse Marilyn told us he had a bad night, with a lot of vomiting and very little sleep even with the medicine. We called Dr. Axlerod who asked which local hospital we routinely used, after getting this information she told us to call an Ambulance to get Joey to the hospital. The doctor called the hospital and made arrangements for Medical Transport to take Joey and Margie to N.YU. Medical Center directly from West Jersey Hospital only 4 or 5 miles from home. I would take the train and meet them at the hospital. Dr. Axlerod got the time from me that my train was due to arrive at Penn Station and had a driver pick me up and drive me to the hospital.

Now we may only be less then a 2 hour drive from New York City, but was still very foreign to us. I had never even been on a real train before, just the Speedline and the Philadelphia Subways, so this was a new experience for me and new experiences were becoming all too common. Joey and his mother arrived atN.Y.U. about an hour before me. When I arrived at Penn Station I wasn't sure how I would find my ride, but when I went outside the terminal there was a man standing beside a big new Lincoln Town holding a cardboard sigh with my name on it (just like in the movies). The driver helped me with our bags and once in the car he told me that my wife and son had arrived safely and how to find them once in the hospital.

I had only been walking through the building a few minutes when I saw Margie in the hallway, I caught up with her and found she was on her way to admissions to get Joey formally admitted. Once the admission process was complete, she took me to the Intensive Care Unit where Joey was. Dr. Axlerod was personally starting an IV (to most doctors starting IV's is a nurses job) to give Joey both fluids and medication. After the IV was started the doctor asked us if we could each go to the blood bank and give a pint of directed donor blood for Joey's surgery. This created an unanticipated problem, Margie's bout with Hepatitis when she was a child eliminated her ability to donate. I asked the doctor if would be possible to donate two pints myself? I was told that a simple blood test would show if l had enough Red Blood Cells and volume to do this safely. After the test it was determined that I could donate two pints at one time if l agreed to an IV running in the other arm to keep my overall volume up, needless to say my stubborn male pride would not allow me to say no.

I went to the blood bank to donate, one bag of iV fluids and two pints of blood later I went back to the ICU with my wife and son, feeling a little weak and tired, but really no worse for wear. After sitting for a short while we took our bags and checked into the Hotel across the street called the Bay View Inn. We unpacked and went back to be with Joey who was now sleeping comfortably from the medication. After another hour or so we got dinner and went back to our room for some much needed rest.

The next two days went by quickly with a lot of Pre-Op testing, for the surgery that was scheduled for mid-morning on Wednesday. The big day came and my wife and I finally met the surgeon, Dr. Howard Ginsberg who was young and we were told very capable. He explained what he would be doing and answered our questions, he was very nice and seemed very confidant about the procedure. All the while Margie and I once again experienced the conflicting emotions of hope and fear at the same time. We hoped that the surgery would be successful, but we also feared our son's ability to survive, especially after being told he was such a high risk patient by the doctors at Children's Hospital of Philadelphia.

As planned Joey was taken to the Operating Room mid-morning on Wednesday and we sat waited and worried for three and a half hours until Dr. Ginsberg came to the room and told us that the surgery was done and our son did just fine (they all use the same words) and he was safely waking up in the recovery room.

When Joey came back to his bed in ICU he was sleeping, there were three bags of fluid and medications along with a pint of my blood running through his IV. I remember joking with the nurses that Joey was getting a pint of the finest Dei go Red available anywhere in the world. Our little boy slept for most of the day, waking up for only a few minutes at a time, which we understood, after all he had just been through the most brutal surgery of his life. I personally knew just how brutal this surgery could be from scrubbing for the same procedure when I worked in the Operating Room at Underwood Memorial.

Later that day Dr. Axlerod introduced Margie and I to a Dr. Kolodney, who was a Harvard professor of Neurology and working on a research grant at N. Y.U. to study the effects o fEndorphin in the Spinal Fluid. Dr. Kolodney told us he had been successful getting children with problems similar to Joey's off of ventilators and help them live fuller, richer lives. He was able to do this by treating them with a drug called Narc an, that is primarily used to reverse the life threatening effects of a narcotic overdose. It turns out that Endorphin's and Narcotics like Morphine or Codeine cause similar reactions in the brain and both are capable of causing the symptoms Joey has had to learn to live with. Unfortunately we would have to wait about a month for the naturally elevated level of Endorphin to drop down to a more normal level due to the surgical trauma his body just experienced. The next day Joey got the last pint of blood I donated and I felt great having been able to meet this need for him. Everything seemed to be going well with some minor exceptions and they were due to the I CU doctors and nurses not understanding Joey's bazaar disease and his unusual need for the ventilator. Dr. Axlerod was very helpful in this respect by explaining the nature of a disease that has never been seen before.

Thursday morning Dr. Axlerod told us that she would like to change the type of ventilator Joey was using, she wanted him to use a volume ventilator instead of the pressure vent he currently used. The doctor explained that the volume vent would be portable and able to be powered by a battery and enable us more freedom with Joey. Margie and I thought this was a great idea provided it would meet our son' s needs. We were assured that it would not only meet Joey's needs but overall it would do less damage to his lungs then the pressure vent would. To this we agreed and the doctor called our equipment company to order the new equipment.

Saturday morning came and Joey was doing much better, he was fighting with the doctors and nurses in his usual defiant manner. As parents we would have liked Joey to be well behaved, but we were always happy to see him fighting, for us this meant there was no question of his survival because he was still fighting to win. Later that afternoon Margie and I left for home on the train, with the intention of returning early the next day. Sunday morning we drove back to N.Y.U. so Margie could be with Joey for the remainder of his stay, we took Mark, Jr and our friend Billy along so they could visit with Joey. Sunday afternoon arrived too quickly and we had to return home, leaving my wife behind.

Once home it was time to return to work Monday morning and try to resume some normalcy. Upon my return to work I was inundated with questions from all my coworkers and most of the doctors. I felt very fortunate to be able to tell them that everything was going smoothly and the surgery was successful and Joey would start to be feed clear liquids via the Gastrostomy tube that day. If he did well with the clear liquids he would resume his regular feeding routine the following day and be discharged for home on Wednesday. I had no way of knowing there would be a hitch that would delay his discharge.

Monday afternoon Margie called work to tell me there had been a problem the night before that may cause his stay in New York to be extended an extra week. It turns out that the IV Joey had running in his foot had come out of the vein (called an IV infiltration) and the IV nutrition called TPN had gotten into the surrounding tissue causing a third degree chemical bum. By 3:30 that afternoon I was on my way back to New York.

When I arrived I checked on Joey and talked to Margie to get as much information as possible, I then demanded to see the head nurse along with all the nursing notes to go along with the incident. I learned that there were a number of problems, first the TPN was running into a shallow peripheral vein instead of a deep vein and a long IV catheter. This was a very basic National Standard of Care that was completely overlooked. Second, thru the night the IV pump gave an occlusion alarm, because Joey did not complain of pain the nurse reset the pump without first checking the IV site on his foot and continued to pump this caustic fluid into the tissues around the vein that inevitably caused a very serious burn.

Armed with this information I had a meeting with the doctors and a Administrative Executive, the doctors wanted to keep Joey an extra week to complete a course of IV Antibiotics to ensure he would not get an infection at the burn site. I was having a problem with this, after all if everyone had done their job properly, this entire incident would not have occurred. I also made clear that while everything was being done to avoid more problems it was creating an expense that we could not afford, with an extra week in New York. To this they offered to pay for Margie's room and meals, while this was helpful, it did nothing to solve the problems of my caring for Mark, Jr while trying to work. Plus the fact that I was getting sick, probably from giving too much blood a week before. Not to mention the extra care being provided, was at the expense of our insurance, it was time to make a deal. I countered that we had run IV's at home in the past and the wound care would be provided by a very competent Plastic Reconstructive surgeon at home. I also told them that we all knew this was a blatant Malpractice, that I would not pursue, provided N.Y.U. paid all the expenses for the Antibiotics and IV therapy as well as all of the follow up wound care. After some discussion it was agreed that Joey's stay would be extended until Saturday and our insurance would not be billed for the extra expenses for their mistake. I can imagine that most people might call this nit picking but with Joey's overall expenses costing between $150,000.00 and $300,000.00 a year this $1,000,000.00 policy could be spent in as little as 4 to 5 years, so in that respect I called it buying time. By early evening I was headed home, hoping it would be my last trip until Saturday when it was time to pick up my wife and child to come home.

Tuesday was my day off so I used it to contact the Respiratory Therapist (Guy) who made sure all of Joey's respiratory needs were being met at home to discuss this new ventilator. Guy explained that he was taking the new vent to N.Y.U. to get it set up for him that afternoon and Joey would use it for the remainder of his stay to ensure a smooth transition to the new machine. We also made arrangements to talk later in the week to hammer out the details for teaching us how use this new equipment when Joey came home.

Now I know this has to sound crazy but the additional problem with Joey being burned seemed to reenforce what had become normal for us. Throughout the first week I was silently waiting for the next shoe to drop, everything was going too good and somehow I knew it was probably too good to be true and it was. We watched problems come from nowhere, at some of the best hospitals in the world and for me at least, I was walking on eggshells wondering what would come next. At least this was a relatively small problem and easily corrected with little or no lifelong implications, other then a Silver Dollar sized scar on Joey's foot. Now the second shoe hit the floor and I could breath a little easier because we had our problem out of the way and this hitch was only an extra two nights. Thursday morning I called and talked to my wife before work and she insisted everything was okay, but she sounded depressed. Margie would not admit it but she was becoming homesick so after work I got Mark and drove up to the hospital for a quick surprise visit to· sooth all of our aching hearts. Three and a half hours round trip driving for an hour visit seemed crazy but it was worth it for the comfort we could find only in each other.

When I got home that night I had a message to call Guy at home regardless of the time. When I called Guy he told me to try to get Joey discharged Friday night instead of Saturday morning because of a huge snow storm due to hit our area late Friday or early Saturday. I told Guy that this was New Jersey and we hear the same story year after year and never get more then a dusting. Guy told me to watch the Weather Channel and see for myself It turned out to be a very large and heavy Noreaster headed our way, for anyone living on the east coast we all knew that Noreaster's where bad and in New Jersey they are the only storms that normally dump large amounts of snow in this area. Upon seeing this I had to change some plans or risk not getting my wife and son home until sometime the following week.

I called my boss at home and told her about the impending storm and asked if I could take the day off to make arrangements to get my family home, she told me to take the day have a safe trip and she will see me Monday at work. Friday morning I called and talked to Dr. Axlerod about getting Joey home that night, to this there was no problem. I called the nursing agency to see if we could get a nurse to go with me to the hospital to get all the orders straight, this too was no problem. I called Guy and told him I would be going to get Joey as soon as the nurse arrived at seven o'clock that evening. He told me about all the equipment I had to bring home with our son so I rented a van. I called Margie and told her to get everything done for the discharge and we would be there around nine o'clock that night. I called Guy back to arrange meeting him back at our house so he could teach us how to use the new vent, I was to call him at home from the last rest area on the New Jersey Turnpike before our exit.

As planned we left home shortly after seven o'clock that night and got to the hospital at N.Y.U. around nine. While Joey's home care nurse

Marilyn, wrote orders and notes Mark, Jr and I started taking equipment to the van. After four loads of stuff we finally had all the equipment loaded and after finalizing the discharge orders and paperwork we left for home around eleven o'clock. By now the heavy New York City traffic nightmare had subsided and little more then an hour and a half we were at the rest area calling Guy and getting some coffee for the little drive we had left. By now it was snowing pretty hard and we were all happy to be near home.

When we got home it was around one o'clock in the morning and Guy was there waiting for us. Once we unloaded the van we had about an hours training with the new equipment, we had to learn how to trouble shoot the different alarms, how to change the tubing that connects to Joey's Trach, how to work the humidifier and how to adjust the ventilator settings. When Guy left it was two or two thirty in the morning and we already had four to six inches of snow on the ground. Guy told us if we had any problems with the new equipment to call him at home.

Finally we were all home and together once again with a major snowstorm falling, our child with new equipment that we didn't know very well and getting IV antibiotics. But somehow with all the unknown problems that might come up, there's still a special feeling that comes when a man's family is home together the way it should be.

When it finally stopped snowing we had eighteen to twenty one inches on the ground and the local TV news and Newspapers were all saying this was the storm of the century. The rest of the weekend went by without incident and the life we now called normal continued just as it always did in the past.

Chapter 8

April arrived and our latest hurdle was behind us, but now we were back to Joey wrenching with dry heaves unable to vomit and we were beginning to wonder if getting this surgery was a mistake. The medicine we were giving him wasn't working anymore and either did the two medications that followed. Our son was suffering through this ordeal by withdrawing emotionally and I was beginning to think I only prolonged the inevitable and caused our boy only more suffering, with little relief. By now Joey had been through two or three short stays at Children's Hospital before we finally met a doctor with an idea.

This doctor was about as arrogant as they come, but at least he was willing to try to help Joey, but this came with the emotional price of a long stay at the Children's Seashore House on the Children's Hospital Campus in Philadelphia. Even though this doctor wasn't very likeable we agreed to this admission and Joey's stay started immediately.

The Children's Seashore House was very new facility in Philadelphia, but had been around for the better part of a century somewhere near Atlantic City and Margie and I where somewhat familiar with the things they did. I think if someone had suggested Voodoo, I think we might have tried it, that's how desperate we felt. After about a month of trying many different treatments the doctor suggested that we try something a Gastrojejunostomy tube to get the feeds further into Joey's small intestine. The up side was that this could be done in Radiology by slipping the tube through the Gastrostomy he already has and using x-ray while sliding the tube into this portion of his intestine.

There was a definite down side, Joey's feeds would last about sixteen hours a day because the tube is very small in diameter, again we agreed.

The doctor scheduled the procedure for the following day and my wife and I could only hope that we might have finally found a treatment. When the time came for our son to get this new tube I was allowed to stay with him throughout the process. I remember being surprised at the apparent inability to comfortably sedate our son, but not for a lack of trying. In his room about a half hour before going to x-ray Joey was given 500mg of Chloral hydrate, which' is a relatively potent sedative along with 50mg of Benydryl, this did nothing. Then during the procedure Joey was fighting a little too much so the doctor gave him a total of 5mg of Versed, which is a very powerful sedative commonly used in the operating room for certain procedures. I have personally gotten the same dose of Versed and at more then 200 pounds I slept like a baby, but with Joey at just over 45 pounds it did nothing, he just refused to be sedated. After the tube was in place and secured we were back in our sons room and I was wondering why these drugs wouldn't work. I asked this new doctor if this might be a clue to his underlying disease that was still undiagnosed. After about fifteen minutes of medical rhetoric and non answers the doctor finally admitted that he didn't know how the medicine worked or why it wouldn't work for Joey, that he only knew the safe dose guidelines. As you might have guessed I'm not the kind of guy that settles for "I don't know" without at least some research, so I looked for some answers on my own.

When we got home that day I called work and talked to one of our Anesthesiologist's named Donna and asked if she would look at a Versed box and tell me who the manufacturer was and where they are located, she told me it is Roche-Pharma in San Juan, Puerto Rico. Donna asked if everything was okay and if she might be able to help? I explained what was going on and how Joey had no response to the drugs he was given that day. Donna being the fine doctor that she is told me there are several reasons why any drug might not work and I was probably on the right track by calling the manufacturer and talking to clinical support.

After hanging up from Donna I called 800 information and got a toll free number for Roche-Pharma in Puerto Rico, I then called and asked for clinical support. A very helpful man that I'm guessing was one of their researchers or scientists talked with me. I told him who I was and I was a parent, not a doctor. I then explained what had happened earlier that day and asked what was to me a simple question. Do you know if this problem has been encountered before and what is the most likely reason for this drug to have no clinical effect? The answer was to say the least startling, it turns out that while this very rarely occurs, there is some research that points to elevated levels of Endorphin in the Cerebral-Spinal Fluid (CFS) which is the fluid that surrounds the brain and spinal cord. If you remember Dr. Kolodney the professor from Harvard, wanted to do a lumbar puncture or spinal tap to look for elevated levels of this very hormone, but could not because of the surgery he just had. Now I had an answer and possibly a clue as to why our sons brain wasn't able to process the things it needs to process so he can function properly and use our senses to fee~ touch and experience life in the way we call normal.

The next day at the Seashore House I told this arrogant doctor that thinks he already knows all the medicine anyone will ever need why the Versed didn't work. I also reminded him that his profession is called a practice because a good doctor is never ready to stop learning. I asked about getting the spinal tap done to look for the suspected elevated Endorphin level. The doctor told me that we don't experiment with children, I explained about the research project at N. Y.U . led by Dr. Kolodney and the success he had been having. To which I was told that if I wanted my son to be part of that research to take him back to New York, so now I had a new hurdle to cross.

Joey was being feed via the new tube and it wasn't looking too promising, he was continuing to wrench, on his side with his knees drawn up to his chest as withdrawn as ever. After three or four days Joey decided he didn't want the new tube anymore and pulled it out, so we were back to square one. The solution was finally found and it was a simple changing of the formula and how he would be fed. Joey would now get this new formula called Jevity and he would be fed slowly through the night, with his feed ending two hours before he normally woke up, to give his stomach time to empty. The plan worked and once again we were able to take our son home after more then two months at the Seashore House.

Once home I started working on getting that last test done to look for the elevated Endorphin in his CFS, unfortunately this was not meant to be. Our insurance would not cover out of state care for experiential proposes. I was told that a spinal tap could be done anywhere so there is no need to go to N.Y.U., the problem was that no doctor that was not connected to this research program was willing to do a Lumbar Puncture for an experiential test they knew nothing about, which led to the ultimate catch 22.

This was 11 years ago and it turned out to be Joey's last long term hospitalization to date. Our son has been frighteningly stable ever since his stay at the Children's Seashore House in Philadelphia, with the exception of a few minor hospital stays for Pneumonia and other respiratory infections. Joey now has a doctor that both his mother and I trust and he is willing to explain things we need explained. Dr. Brigila, MD. has made a career specializing in multiply disabled children and because he understands the difficulty of getting people like Joey out, he makes house calls and he is a truly dying breed.

Closing Thoughts

That last stay at the Children's Seashore House was in 1993, Joey was 7 years old and Margie and I were thinking about the prognosis of our son not living past 8. It is now 2004 and Joey turned 18 November 5, 2003, Joey is totally dependent on the ventilator to breathe, he is now in a wheel chair too, having not been able to walk since he was 14 years old. He still goes to school daily with a nurse to care for him and he's still living at home where he belongs. Mark Jr. is now married to with a son named Ethan and a daughter on the way. Margie has gone back to school to learn how to draw blood for testing, DNA cell collection and EKG's, she has worked in a hospital for 4 years and now works for a private lab doing house calls to do blood tests for people that cannot get out. I am back to driving trucks locally and still trying to live the American Dream.

It has been over seventeen years since Joey first got sick and I personally have learned many tough lessons that I am grateful to have learned, the fact that the learning process was tough made these lessons all the more valuable. The most important lesson I've learned that the valuable things in life can't be bought and true riches can't be spent, basically if your willing to have a family, then they and NOT money should always be the most important thing in your life. Remember when you were told that when you die you can't take your money with you, but I honestly believe that the love that only a family can have, can and will endure all of eternity. The religions that believe in reincarnation, have always taught that your actions and values in this life, will play a major part in the next life, Karma. As a Christian I believe that if you devoted your life to doing the right things in life and probably the most important thing is love and devotion to family, are very important in the long and slow step by step journey to Heaven'

Everybody's journey through life has always started with a single step and at only 45 and 8 joint surgeries later, I feel older then I ever expected to be and while death no longer causes me any fear, I somehow still look forward to tomorrow. I personally refuse to take undue credit for Joey's survival thus far, because Joey was the one doing the real fighting, all that anyone else could do was to help him to want to keep fighting, and giving him the love it takes to win. This does not mean I haven't accomplished much because I have, the most important is still and God willing will always be having a family to love, that gives me love in return.

I've also learned that when thing aren't going the way you hoped they would go, but you already have what I have, then you already have it all. I am very proud of both of my children, Mark Jr husband and parent himself, he stands tall and does the right thing for his family. Joey has defied all the odds and grew to be a proud young man while teaching his father the most important lessons he would ever learn and he did that without ever really talking. My beautiful wife Margie has over come a severe brain injury and gone back to school to learn something she never had any interest in before Joey, Para Medical Technology. Margie works at a job she loves and is about complete a course to become an EMT, after which she wants to go back to school to become a Paramedic. Like I said I already have it all, I am after all, a very proud husband and father.

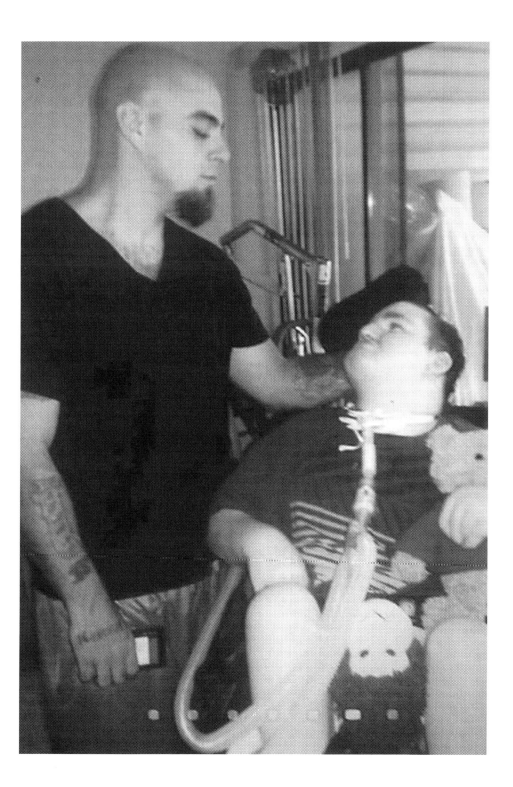

In Remembrance of
Mark J.Gattuso Sr.
Joseph C.Gattuso

The original author of this book is Mark J.Gattuso Sr.

Printed in the United States
By Bookmasters